Acknowledgements

I am grateful to Sarah O'Neill, Legal Officer at the Scottish Consumer Council, for her editorial guidance in revising the first edition of this book.

I would also like to thank members of the conveyancing committee of the Law Society of Scotland, staff at Communities Scotland, the Royal Incorporation of Chartered Surveyors in Scotland, the National House-Building Council, the Council of Mortgage Lenders, Zurich Insurance and the British Association of Removers, Alison Hatrick of the National Association of Estate Agents and Margaret Ross of Aberdeen University for their comments on particular chapters and sections.

Derek Manson-Smith
February 2006

About the Scottish Consumer Council

The Scottish Consumer Council (SCC) was set up by government in 1975. Our purpose is to make all consumers matter. We do this by putting forward the consumer interest, particularly that of disadvantaged groups in society, by researching, campaigning and working with those who can make a difference to achieve beneficial change.

While producers of goods and services are usually well-organised and articulate when protecting their own interests, individual consumers very often are not. The people whose interests we represent are consumers of all kinds: they may be patients, tenants, parents, solicitors' clients, public transport users, or simply shoppers in a supermarket.

Consumers benefit from efficient and effective services in the public and private sectors. Service providers benefit from discriminating consumers. A balanced partnership between the two is essential and the SCC seeks to develop this partnership by:

* carrying out research into consumer issues and concerns;

* informing key policy and decision-makers about consumer concerns and issues;

* influencing key policy and decision-making processes;

* informing and raising awareness among consumers.

Part 1
Introduction

1.1. Why move?

Moving home can be a part of one of the more positive events of life, such as being able to afford a better home and standard of living or moving to another part of the country. Unfortunately, it is often associated with one of the more stressful events of life, such as changing job, starting a family, divorce or bereavement.

This book will help to make moving home a less stressful experience for you. It describes the Scottish system of home purchase and sale, looks at the various choices you have and gives guidance about the things to consider when making these choices. It also points out the pitfalls to be avoided at various stages in the process, and provides a checklist of things to remember leading up to the move. We hope it will help you to make the right move.

1.2. Do you really need to move?

Some people might consider the prospect of moving home to be so daunting that they may not want to move at all. It is worth considering whether you really need to move, especially if you are happy where you are. However, it may be that your home no longer suits you because your circumstances have changed since you moved there. Perhaps it is now too small or too big, or you or someone living with you has become disabled, or with increasing years can no longer cope with the layout. It may be that you could make some alterations to your home so that you don't have to move.

If you own your home and feel it is now too small, you could add an extension if you have a big enough garden to build on. If it is too big, it might be worth letting out a room or rooms, or sub-dividing it and selling or renting out a part of it. You might be able to borrow money from the lender who gave you your mortgage to make the alterations.

If your home needs serious repairs done to it, you may be able to get a home improvement grant from your local council. These are discretionary and depend on the age and value of your home. If your home is short of basic necessities, such as a bath or shower, a wash-hand basin, a sink, hot and cold water and a toilet, you may be eligible for a grant to pay for installing these. If you or someone in your family is disabled and your home is short of basic necessities or needs adaptations to make it suitable to live in, you may be able to get a grant from your local council to cover installing the basic necessities or making the adaptations or both.

If you own your home and you or someone in your family is elderly and, because of this, cannot cope with the layout of your home, you could qualify for a grant to make suitable alterations if your council has a care-and-repair scheme.

However, if you don't want to or can't stay where you are, you may want to consider whether you want to rent or buy. Your answer may well depend on whether you are renting your home at the moment, or whether you own it. It is worth considering the advantages and disadvantages of both. While owning your own home has always been considered a worthwhile investment, the rate of increase in house prices in Scotland in the first half of the 2000s has slowed, although the market has always been more stable than that in England and Wales. Home ownership carries with it heavy responsibilities for maintenance of the property, and usually the burden of paying for a mortgage for many years in the future. Renting may be more flexible and better suited to those in more casual employment, or who tend to move from one part of the country to another, and it may be cheaper in the long run.

If you are getting older, you may wish to consider buying or renting some kind of sheltered accommodation. This book does not cover sheltered accommodation, but you can find details of where to go for more information about this at 1.3 below.

If you own your home and decide to move, you will need to decide whether it is best to buy a new home or sell your existing home first. This will depend on your circumstances and you should discuss them with your solicitor.

1.3. Further information

If you want to find out more about care and repair in your area, you should contact your local authority housing department. You can also contact the Care and Repair Forum, 236 Clyde Street, Glasgow G1 4JH (tel: 0141 221 9879, e-mail: forum@care-repair-scot.org.uk)

Access to housing in Scotland: rights for disabled people. Available free of charge from: HomePoint, Communities Scotland, Thistle House, 91 Haymarket Terrace, Edinburgh EH12 5HE (tel: 0131 313 0044, e-mail: homepoint@communitiesscotland.gsi.gov.uk).

Buying retirement housing, Factsheet 2S, which includes sheltered accommodation, is available free of charge from Age Concern, Freepost (SWB 30375), Ashburton, Devon TQ13 7ZZ, (tel: 0800 00 99 66 or download from http://www.ageconcernscotland.org.uk/pdf.pl?file=age/news/FS2sJUL05.pdf).

Part 2

What are you looking for?

2.1. What can you afford?

At the end of the day, it may be that cost is the deciding factor in whether you rent a furnished home, rent an unfurnished home or buy a home. The decision is yours but if you decide to buy, you should consider the essential costs that should be included in your budget.

You can use this table to help you work out the essential costs.

Table 2.1. Costs of buying and owning a home

One-off costs	£
Deposit towards purchase price	
Mortgage arrangement fee	
Mortgage indemnity guarantee (high lending fee)[1]	
Surveyor's fees	
Solicitor's fees and expenses	
Stamp duty land tax [2]	
Registration fees	
Removal	
Furniture etc	
Telephone or cable reconnection	
Total	

[1] Some lenders may require this if you are borrowing more than 75 per cent to 80 per cent of the purchase price

[2] Where the purchase price is more than £125,000

Continuing costs	£
Factor's or common charges [3]	
Mortgage payments/life insurance premiums	
Mortgage payment protection insurance	
Buildings insurance premiums	
Contents insurance premiums	
Exterior repairs and maintenance costs	
Interior repairs and maintenance costs	
Electricity bills	
Gas bills	
Telephone bills	
Internet/broadband/cable bills	
Council tax, water and sewerage charges	
Total	

[3] If you live in a block of flats or tenement

2.2. Where do you want to live?

There is a combination of factors that could affect where you want to live.

• City, town or countryside? There are advantages and disadvantages to each. A city or town offers more choice of housing, services and social life. On the other hand, compared with the countryside, your environment may be more polluted and crowded, home prices and insurance rates may be higher, and services and public transport may be poor in some parts of cities. You can also feel isolated and lonely in a city. The countryside may offer a better environment, more possibilities for a garden or land, lower insurance costs and an easier pace of life. On the other hand, compared with city or town life, the countryside can be cut off in winter, there is less choice of housing, and services, leisure facilities and public transport may be poor or non-existent. You also have less choice of social activities and it may take a while to become accepted into the local community. If you work in a town or city and want to live in the countryside, you should think about how much time you want to spend commuting.

- Do you need to live close to where you work? If not, you will have a wider choice of neighbourhoods.

- Do you have children? Schools and access to leisure activities are an important consideration if you have children of school age.

- Do you have your own transport? If you are dependent on public transport, you will want to know that services are available and reliable.

2.3. What type of home do you want?

This will depend largely on what you can afford to buy. Within your budget, you should consider:

- The space you want. Are large rooms important, or the number of them? Do you want a garden and, if so, do you want one that needs lots of upkeep?

- Whether you want to live on one level or at ground level or both. A bungalow or ground-floor flat may be more appropriate for you if you are elderly or have a disability. If you don't mind living at the top of a tenement now, how will you feel if you later have young children or when you get older?

- How long you would expect to live in this home, the area or part of the country.

- How your circumstances might change in the future; for example, if you have children you may want more space.

2.4. New or old?

If you decide to buy a home, and depending on where you want to live, you have a choice of buying a newly-built or newly-converted home from a builder or developer or one that has been lived in. A new home has the advantages that:

- you are literally making a new start;

- it may be easier to get a mortgage;

- you are not dependent on someone else selling their home;

- the builder may be prepared to make some changes to suit you before it is finished;

- you can choose your own decoration;

- the price you pay may include extras, such as new carpets, curtains, a fitted kitchen and appliances;

- the property will carry a structural warranty or guarantee if the builder is registered with the National House-Building Council (NHBC), Zurich Insurance or Premier Guarantee (see 4.4.1);

- the builder may offer to take your current home in part exchange;

- the builder may offer a shared equity arrangement, which may make it easier for you to buy. For example, if a home costs £140,000 and the builder retains a 20 per cent share, you would pay £112,000. If you later sold it for £180,000, you would get £144,000 and the builder would get £36,000.

The disadvantages are:

- you may not have a choice as to when the home will be ready for you to move in;

- there may be teething problems ('snagging') while the building settles in;

- you may have to spend time and money fitting and equipping it;

- you may have to do a lot of work to turn a building site into a garden;

- you may have to make stage payments (see 4.4) as the home is built and so end up borrowing to pay for two homes at the same time (see 5.6);

- extras, such as a cooker and fridge freezer, may be included in the price of the property when you buy it. If you decide to sell your home within a short time of buying it, the valuation will not include the value of these extras, which might mean that you get less than you paid for the home.

Buying a home that has been lived in will avoid these disadvantages. If it is less than 10-years old, it should still be covered by an NHBC warranty or a Premier Guarantee or if less than 15-years old by a Zurich Insurance warranty, if it was built by a builder registered under one of these schemes. The advantages of buying an older home are that:

- you will be moving into an established neighbourhood;

- you are more likely to have amenities such as shops, schools and public transport.

A disadvantage of an older home is that the upkeep costs of decoration, repairs and maintenance are likely to be higher than with a new home.

In the end, however, the decision on whether to buy new or old is often simply a matter of personal taste.

2.5. Living and storage space

Your home is not just for sleeping and eating in. Everyone will need their own space, and over time, the needs of your family will change. The needs of a three-year old are different from those of an eight-year old or a thirteen-year old.

The way your home is divided up can help you live the way you want or make living together difficult. An open-plan living area can make a small home appear more spacious, but it does not provide much privacy. Separate dining and living rooms can compensate for a lack of space in bedrooms to study or relax in. But this could mean that the rooms are quite small and it could be difficult to arrange furniture.

You should consider what you will need to store and where you will store it. As well as built-in storage, you will need space for free-standing furniture, shelving and coat racks and you will want the storage space to be in the right place. Where would you store the following?

clothes	cleaning materials
bed linen	ironing board
toys	dirty laundry
suitcases	sewing machine
outdoor clothes	fresh food
boots and shoes	frozen food
umbrellas	tinned food
baby buggy or pram	bulk-buy items
a stepladder	crockery
DIY tools and supplies	pots and pans
videos, CDs and DVDs	pet food and cat litter
books	coal or wood for an open fire
sports equipment	kitchen refuse
hobby equipment	papers, bottles and other
bicycles	materials for recycling
vacuum cleaner	garden tools
broom	

Part 3

Buying a home: making a decision

3.1. Introduction

Scotland has its own legal system and law governing the ownership of land and property. Most residential property is sold on the basis that the buyer gains the right to occupy and use it for as long as they own it. The concepts of leasehold and freehold found elsewhere in the United Kingdom do not generally apply in Scotland.

In Scotland, you make a written offer to buy and the seller accepts it in writing. A number of letters, known as 'missives', clarifying details and conditions of the offer and acceptance may be exchanged. Once these details are agreed, 'missives are concluded' and you have a binding contract (see 4.2). Should you be unable to fulfil your obligations in the missives, you may be liable to the seller for damages of thousands of pounds. Therefore, before making an offer, you must get legal advice and arrange the finance to meet the purchase price (see 5.2).

Until missives are concluded, it is possible for either the buyer or seller to withdraw without penalty, although this rarely happens in practice. Once the missives are concluded, however, you will have a binding contract, an agreed date of entry (see 4.2), and you cannot be 'gazumped'.

This is different from the situation in England, Wales and Northern Ireland, where someone wishing to buy a home makes an offer to buy 'subject to contract', which is not binding on either party. If this is accepted, he or she then has to find the funds to pay the price and the solicitors or conveyancers for both sides will check the title and draw up formal contract documents. When the parties are satisfied, formal contracts of sale are exchanged. Until this point, either party can withdraw without penalty and the seller could accept a better offer from a different prospective buyer. This is known as 'gazumping'.

The legal aspects of buying a home are explained in more detail in Chapter 4.

3.2. Buying your rented home

If you are a Scottish secure tenant of a council (including a housing management cooperative), a housing association or other registered social landlord (that is registered with Communities Scotland) or a water authority, you may have a legal right to buy your home at a discount. This does not include accommodation provided under a contract of employment, that is, tied housing, certain temporary lettings, and homeless accommodation.

If you are unsure about whether you currently have a right to buy, you should check with your landlord.

The main requirements are:

• you must normally have spent at least two or five years (depending on when your tenancy started) as a secure tenant immediately before making the application;

• the home you rent must be occupied by you as your only or main home.

You need not have lived in the same home or had the same landlord all the time. For example, you can also count time spent as a tenant of certain other bodies, such as the armed forces, a water authority or the Forestry Commission.

If your tenancy dates back to before 30 September 2002 and it allowed you to exercise the right to buy, the old terms and conditions will continue to apply to the right to buy for as long as you remain in that tenancy. However, with some limited exceptions, if your tenancy started on or after 30 September 2002 then the new terms associated with the modernised right to buy will apply. This is known as a 'preserved right to buy'.

You cannot buy your home if:

- you do not have a Scottish secure tenancy or a preserved right to buy;

- you rent from a charitable housing association, which normally would have obtained charitable status before 18 July 2001, unless you had a right to buy as a tenant of the landlord before 30 September 2002;

- your landlord has fewer than 100 homes;

- your home has special features for elderly people;

- it is part of a group housing scheme for people with special needs where the tenants have special facilities for their use or they are provided with housing support services or both;

- it is required by an islands council for accommodation connected with education;

- your home forms part of a fully-mutual cooperative housing association;

- your home is earmarked for demolition and your landlord has obtained a consent to refuse to sell;

- you rent from a council that has been granted 'pressured-area status' and your tenancy started after 30 September 2002.

In addition, your landlord may refuse to sell if you have arrears of rent, council tax, water and sewerage charges, or other amounts owing as a result of your current or a previous tenancy, or if your landlord is in the process of evicting you because of your conduct.

Contacts for further information on buying your rented home are given at 3.14.

3.3. Other options

Shared ownership

Some housing associations and private developers operate a shared ownership scheme, where the home is owned jointly by the landlord and tenant. You buy a share in the home (25 per cent, 50 per cent or 75 per cent of the purchase price) and pay rent on the balance. You can buy additional 25 per cent shares once a year, so that you eventually own the home, or you can carry on renting.

Homestake

If you are on a low income and cannot afford the price of a home, this scheme allows you to share a stake (normally between 60 per cent and 80 per cent) of the market value of a property, with the option for increasing it to 100 per cent later. The scheme is similar to shared ownership (see above), except that you will own the property outright and do not have to pay rent on the balance. For further information, see 3.14.

Rural Home Ownership Grants

If you live and work in a rural area and are a first-time buyer or you are a pensioner, sick or disabled and have a local family connection, and cannot afford to buy a home, you may qualify for a Rural Home Ownership Grant towards the cost of buying or building a home. For further information, see 3.14.

Crofter Housing Grants and Loans

If you are a registered crofter, you may be able to get a grant or loan to help you with the costs of building a new croft house or of improving an existing croft house. The Scottish Executive Environment and Rural Affairs Department administers the scheme. For further information, see 3.14.

Cash-incentive scheme

If you are a tenant of a council or registered social landlord you may qualify for a grant towards the purchase of a home in the private sector. Some councils operate cash-incentive schemes that aim to free up council accommodation for re-letting to others in housing need while providing financial assistance to aspiring homeowners. To find out more about the scheme, contact your landlord.

3.4. Where to look for homes for sale

3.4.1. New homes

If you want to buy a new home, you should contact a builder directly or the builder's sales agent. They normally advertise in local newspapers, on television, on the Internet, sometimes through solicitors, and in *Scotland's New Homebuyer*, which is a free quarterly publication available from building societies, solicitors' property centres, and selected banks and estate agents.

3.4.2. Older homes

If you want to buy an older home, there are three main sources of information.

Newspapers

Most homes for sale are advertised in local newspapers by estate agents, solicitors and private individuals. Daily papers usually have a set day for property advertisements and some publish a weekly supplement.

Estate agents

Remember that the estate agent is working for the seller, not for you, the prospective purchaser. This is the case even if the agent offers to provide other services, such as to help you find a mortgage. It is a good idea to contact local estate agents in the area and give them details of the type of home you are looking for and the price range you can afford. You can get details of any homes they have on offer and get on their postal and e-mail lists for details of homes that come onto the market later. The larger agents publish details of properties throughout Scotland in free news-sheets and on their websites. An estate agent will usually arrange for you to view likely homes and, if you are interested, will negotiate with you on behalf of the seller.

Solicitors' property centres

Scottish solicitors have a long-standing tradition of selling property. Solicitors' property centres act for solicitors who subscribe to them. You should contact local property centres and give them details of the type of home you are looking for and the price range you can afford. They keep details of properties on offer and maintain mailing lists for homes coming onto the market. The larger property centres publish free news-sheets that list all the properties offered for sale by their subscribing solicitors. If you register your requirements on their websites, you will be sent details of suitable properties by e-mail. You can find details of solicitors' property centres on the Scottish Solicitors' Property Centres website at http://www.sspc.co.uk/. Usually, viewing will be arranged through the solicitor working for the seller, and the property details will include information on viewing. Any subsequent negotiations are conducted with the selling solicitor. Remember that, as is the case with an estate agent, the solicitor who is selling the property through a property centre is working for the seller, not you.

3.5. Property descriptions

It is important to gather all the information you can about any property you are interested in. The Property Misdescriptions Act 1991 makes it an offence for an estate agent, a builder or a solicitor to give any description of a property that is not truthful, although it does not make any rules on the topics covered or the amount of detail. If you believe that you have been given any information that is misleading or untruthful, you can refer it to your local trading standards or environmental services department (see under the entry for your local council in the phone book). If a builder or agent is successfully prosecuted under the Act, you may be able to sue for damages.

From 2008, the seller or the seller's agent must provide you with a survey report and other information about the property. Guidance on how the system will work will be available nearer the time.

New homes

Most builders provide useful information about new homes. If you plan to buy a new home, you should make sure that you get the following information:

- A leaflet with floor plans and dimensions: this will give you an idea of how the rooms are arranged.

- A plan of the site layout: this will give you an idea of the size of the site. It can also help you choose the location of a home on the site if it has not yet been built and may tell you something about parking and road safety.

- A specification sheet: this will describe the type of walls, doors, windows, kitchen and bathroom fittings.

Older homes

Solicitors' property centres and estate agents do not normally provide plans but they usually provide a property description. If you are responding to an advertisement placed by a private seller, you may not get any written information. If you do receive any written information or a purchaser's information pack from a private seller, remember that it is not controlled by the Property Misdescriptions Act. A property description will give you a general idea of the property, which should help you decide whether it is worth viewing. The dimensions given are usually only approximate so, if they are important to you, you should check them on site. It is important to check the description carefully to see what is included, such as cookers, carpets, curtains, and so on. If you later make an offer to buy, you should make sure that these items are specified in the offer by your solicitor.

From 2008, if you are buying from your council or registered social landlord under your right to buy, your landlord will have to give you information about the maintenance costs of the property and common parts and the life expectancy of the common parts, fixtures and fittings and their replacement costs.

3.6. Viewing

Before you view a home, you should think about the things that are important to you. The following list gives some suggestions:

- the neighbourhood – local amenities, such as schools, places of worship, shops and public transport, and neighbouring properties;
- car parking;
- space for children to play;
- gardens and balconies;
- safety and security;
- open-plan living space or separate rooms;
- fittings, fixtures and equipment – what you need that may be included and what you will be wanting to take with you;
- storage space;
- the layout of rooms;
- noise from neighbours;
- daylight and views;
- heating costs;
- council tax band;
- broadband access, cable television connections or satellite dish;
- whether old lead piping has been replaced;
- alterations that have been done or that you may wish to do (see 3.7);
- in the case of flats, whether the building is managed by the owners or a property manager or factor.

Draw up a checklist of things that are important to you. It will help you think methodically about your needs, remind you about things you may easily forget, and help you decide which features are most important.

When you view properties, keep a record of those you visit and make notes on the property description. Collect as much information as you can so that you can read through it later.

If you are interested in a particular property, you should visit the neighbourhood and the home again during the day and at night, on a weekday and a weekend. They may seem very different at different times.

3.7. Alterations

3.7.1. Alterations made by the seller or previous owner

If the seller or a previous owner has made any alterations to a property you want to buy, these may have needed planning permission or building control consent or both. Some properties that have special character may also be listed as of special architectural or historic interest: changes to these buildings need listed building consent. There may also be conditions in the title deeds that prohibit alterations that have been made. Your solicitor should enquire about alterations and, where these have been made, ensure that any necessary permission, building warrants, consents and completion certificates have been granted. If any permission, warrant, consent or certificate has not been obtained that should have been, you could be faced with very expensive work to meet the conditions or undo the work. So, make sure that your solicitor makes these enquiries.

3.7.2. Alterations you may want to make

If you are planning to make alterations to a property you are going to buy, you should find out whether you need, and can get, permission before you make an offer as this could affect your decision to buy.

It is very important to make sure that any planning consents, building warrants and completion certificates are placed with the title deeds for safekeeping, as you will need to provide these when you sell the property in the future.

Planning permission

You will not need planning permission for certain minor changes, for example, most loft conversions or dormer windows, hedges, low fences and walls or a satellite dish up to 90 cm in diameter. However, some loft conversions and dormer windows do require planning permission. For some changes, you do not need planning permission, provided certain conditions are fulfilled, for example, small extensions, garages and outhouses. Most porches to the front of a property do require planning permission.

You will need permission or consent or both, even for those changes that do not normally require it, if:

- the property is a listed building (that is, a building listed under the Town and Country Planning (Scotland) Acts as being of special architectural or historic interest);

- the property is in a conservation area (that is, an area designated as of special architectural or historic interest, the character or appearance of which it is desirable to preserve or enhance);

- in other circumstances if conditions have been imposed, restricting the types of changes allowed.

It is important to be absolutely sure about the position, so you should always contact the planning department at your local council before starting any work.

Building control consent

As well as planning permission, you may need building control consent. This takes the form of a warrant (or permission) from the local council building control department certifying that the proposed building work complies with the building standards regulations. For example, you need to have building control approval for internal and external alterations to existing buildings and new or altered drainage systems. Again, you should check beforehand whether the work you are planning to do needs a building control warrant.

You do not need approval for minor work such as general repairs, the installation of fitted wardrobes or electric heaters, or the installation of gas appliances by approved fitters.

Title deeds

The title deeds are the legal documents that set out your rights of ownership of a property, and they may restrict the changes you can make to it. For example, they can prohibit the use of the property for business purposes or specify how the exterior of the building should look.

If you want to do something that is prohibited by a condition in the title deeds, you can apply to the Lands Tribunal for Scotland to change the condition. Your solicitor should be able to do this for you. For more information on the powers of the tribunal and how to make an application, see 3.14.

3.8. Special treatments, guarantees and insurance

Your solicitor should ask for details of any special treatments that have been carried out in the property, such as treatment for wet or dry rot, or the installation of a damp-proof course.

Special treatments should be covered by a guarantee or insurance policy. Make sure that your solicitor checks that any guarantees or insurance policies are valid and can be transferred to you. If the company that provided the guarantee has gone out of business, then it will be useless unless it is backed by insurance. It will also be of little use if the guarantee period is due to run out soon.

If your survey report indicates the need for special treatments, you should ask for a full report, specification and quotation before you decide how much to offer. Most reputable preservation companies will give you a free quotation.

A home that that was built, converted or renovated 10 years ago or less may be covered by a National House-Building Council Buildmark warranty or Premier Guarantee warranty and one that is less than 15 years old may be covered by a Zurich Building Guarantee warranty (see 4.4.1 and 4.4.2). These warranty policies can be transferred to a new owner but they exclude damage or defects that you knew about when you bought the home or which might reasonably have been discovered by a survey. If your survey shows up problems covered by a warranty policy, you should find out if the current owner is prepared to make a claim before you consider making an offer.

Again, you should keep any warranty policy documents with the title deeds.

3.9. Fixtures, appliances and central heating

Any fixtures and appliances included in the purchase price should be in reasonable working order. You should try to find out how old they are, whether they are still under guarantee and, if so, whether the guarantees can be transferred to you.

Central heating systems can cause problems. Find out if there is a maintenance contract or, if there is not, how old the system is and when an engineer last looked at it. If you are having a homebuyer's or building survey done, ask your surveyor to check if the system is working and appears adequate. But remember that the surveyor is not a heating engineer. For peace of mind you may wish to instruct a heating engineer to check the system. Any repairs or replacements could involve considerable expense and you may need to take these into account when deciding how much to offer for the property.

3.10. Running costs

You should find out as much as you can about the running costs of a home before you buy. Details of some of the outgoings should be easy to get. For example, information about council tax, water and sewerage charges will be available from the seller or the seller's agent.

Other costs will depend on your lifestyle. For new homes, the National Home Energy Rating (NHER), which gives you an indication of a house's annual energy costs, may be available if the builder has had an assessment carried out. You could commission an assessment yourself, which would cost between £50 and £150. For an older home (and possibly for a new home), from 2008 you must be given an energy report on the condition and energy efficiency of the property. In the meantime, you could commission an NHER assessment, which would cost between £75 and £200. For more information, see 3.14. You can also get some idea of fuel costs for an older home by asking the seller what the average cost of gas and electricity was for the last year.

The following list includes the main outgoings you should allow for:

• Mortgage payments (see Chapter 5)

• Council tax, water and sewerage charges

• Insurance premiums – contents and buildings (see 3.11 and 3.13.4), mortgage payment protection (see 5.7), life (see 5.8)

• Fuel – electricity and gas, oil, or coal

• Telephone, internet and cable/satellite

• Television licence

• Repairs and redecoration – interior and exterior

• Factor's or service charges (if you live in a flat – see 3.13)

3.11. Insurance

3.11.1. Contents

You are under no obligation to insure the contents of your home. However, a home contents insurance policy, besides covering your belongings, provides valuable additional cover. If your home is badly damaged and you have to move out while repairs are carried out, the policy will usually pay towards the reasonable cost of alternative accommodation. Your legal liability for injury to someone or damage to his or her property while in your home is usually covered, as is your liability in day-to-day life if, for example, as a pedestrian you cause an expensive traffic accident. It is important to shop around for insurance, to check what will be covered, and to read your policy once you receive it to see what is included.

3.11.2. Buildings

While it is strongly advisable, if you buy a detached or semi-detached house you do not have any legal obligation to insure it unless the title deeds require it. However, if you have a mortgage, the lender will insist that you take out buildings insurance covering the reinstatement cost of your home, that is, the full cost of rebuilding the property and not just its current market value. If you buy a flat, you and your fellow owners are legally obliged to insure your own flats for their reinstatement values. Alternatively, you and your fellow owners could agree to meet that obligation by taking out a common insurance policy for the reinstatement value of the whole building. If the building has a factor, there may already be a common insurance policy covering the whole building (see 3.13.4).

Most mortgage lenders offer buildings insurance as part of a package with the mortgage. Normally, you do not have to insure through the lender, but if you buy your insurance elsewhere, your lender may make a small charge for checking that the policy is suitable backing for the loan.

You are responsible for making sure that your insurance cover is adequate. Any significant under-insurance could mean that any claim you make might be reduced or even rejected. Your valuation or survey report will normally contain a recommended amount for buildings insurance.

Buildings insurance, as well as covering the structure together with the fixtures and fittings, also covers your legal liability as the owner. For example, if someone is injured or damage is caused to their property because of your negligence, you could find yourself having to pay damages or compensation, which may amount to a lot of money.

If you live in a flat or share ground or property with other people, your insurance should cover your share of responsibility for common parts (see 3.13.4).

3.12. Potential problems with neighbourhoods and neighbours

3.12.1. The neighbourhood

You can get a good idea of a neighbourhood by visiting it at different times of the day and week before you buy. Consider things like vacant land nearby. This may become the site of a new housing or industrial development. How would this alter the neighbourhood and the view from your home? Other factors to consider are the proximity of things like a pub, a take-away, a school playground or a disco. Would you mind living near these? The neighbourhood may be too noisy for you or there may be heavy traffic congestion or pollution at certain times of the day. Look out for potential problems such as factories and dairies, quarries, goods yards, railway lines and airports and decide whether these may affect you.

Car parking can cause problems, even if you do not own a car. The neighbourhood will be more pleasant to live in if there is adequate parking for residents and visitors. A shortage of parking spaces can lead to disputes between neighbours. In some inner-city areas, car owners have to pay for a resident's parking permit to park outside their homes.

3.12.2. Neighbours

You have to share your neighbourhood with people who may have very different lifestyles to yours. Good neighbours are invaluable, but unsociable neighbours can make life a nightmare. Although you cannot choose your neighbours, you can look for features that reduce the likelihood of problems. These include marked parking spaces for visitors' cars, separate driveways and front paths, doorways that do not face each other directly, and proper bin-storage areas.

If you live in a block of flats, the garden may belong to the ground-floor flat or be shared by other owners. If it is shared and you live on the ground floor, you may have little control over who can use the garden. You may not enjoy a garden full of party-goers or children playing near your windows.

Noise is a major cause of disputes between neighbours. If you can hear your neighbours, they can also hear you. When you look at a home, you should consider:

• the quality of the construction of the home: for example, party walls between flats, terraced and semi-detached houses. In older converted houses, the floors between flats may not provide enough noise insulation;

• the layout, or the way spaces in neighbouring homes are organised: for example, the living room, kitchen, hall and bathroom of a flat on one floor should not lie over bedrooms in the flat below.

It is difficult to do anything about bad neighbours once you move in − except move. So, try to find out before you buy. Ask the seller what the neighbours are like (although if the neighbours are noisy, they are unlikely to tell you), whether they have children or pets, how long have they lived there, and so on.

3.13. Responsibilities of flat owners

Owning a flat is a lot more complicated than owning a house. When you own a house, you only have to look after your own property. When you buy a flat, you also take on a share with the other owners of maintaining the common parts of the building. These can include the roof, the shared entrance, the stairs, a lift (if there is one), the outside walls, the garden and, in some cases, cleaning and caretaking services.

3.13.1. Tenements and multiple-occupancy buildings

Legally, every flat owner has some responsibility towards the repair and maintenance of shared areas and services. This means that you also have to pay your share of the costs. In many cases, the title deeds of the property will set out the common areas of the building you can use and for which you are responsible, what share of the maintenance you pay, how decisions should be reached among the various owners, and whether you have to employ a factor to look after the property.

If there are gaps in the title deeds, such as them not saying how decisions should be taken or not describing all the common parts, or defects, such as allocating shares of costs that do not add up to 100 per cent, then the Tenement Management Scheme will fill the gaps or correct the defects. The scheme is part of the Tenements (Scotland) Act 2004. It does not affect your ownership of your flat. You can find further information in *Common Repair, Common Sense: a homeowner's guide to the management and maintenance of common property* (see 3.14).

Many flats, especially in Glasgow and the West of Scotland, have a factor or property manager to look after repairs and maintenance. This is common in old tenement buildings in Glasgow but is also popular in modern blocks of flats throughout Scotland. Factors are firms that specialise in maintaining multiple-ownership properties. Generally, they will inspect the property at least once a year and arrange for common repairs to be carried out. Individual owners are usually billed either twice or four times a year for the factor's fee and any common repair costs. If large or expensive repairs are required, the factor may insist on the approval of all the owners and ask for advance payment before the work is carried out.

You do not have to have a factor unless it is required by the title deeds or deed of conditions. Provided a majority of the owners agree, you can get together and arrange for maintenance and repairs as necessary. Similarly, provided a majority of the owners agree, you can appoint a factor, or change a factor.

If you buy a new, modern or converted flat, there will usually be a deed of conditions about the development or the building. This sets out what you can and cannot do with your property, for example, whether you can keep pets or restrictions on the decoration of the outside of your property, and may provide for the appointment of a factor.

3.13.2. Former rented flats

If you decide to buy a flat that you have been renting from a public-sector body, such as a council or a registered social landlord (see 3.2), the same general rules apply as to any other flat buyer. The title deeds will set out your rights and duties towards other owners. However, your former landlord may own some of the other flats and, if it owns most of them, it will be able to do repairs and maintenance as and when it decides. As a joint owner, you will be responsible for meeting your share of the costs.

You should be absolutely clear about what you are buying, for example, whether you actually own or share ownership of the garden or drying green (which will mean that you also have to share maintenance costs), or whether you only have rights of access.

3.13.3. Sheltered and retirement housing

Services in sheltered and retirement housing can include shared facilities, such as a lounge, laundry, guest bedrooms, an emergency alarm system or the services of a warden or both. Services include cleaning, maintenance and insurance of the common parts. You pay your share of the costs of amenities and services through a service charge. These charges can be particularly significant and will go up over the years, so it is important to find out as much as you can about them.

3.13.4. Insurance

Adequate insurance is a common property obligation. You are not adequately insured unless you and all your fellow owners in the building are adequately insured. While you are responsible for insuring your own flat, you and your fellow owners are legally obliged to insure your flats for their reinstatement values. When you take out a mortgage, your lender will insist that you have buildings insurance that meets its requirements (see 3.11.2). This should cover damage to your own flat and also your share of the common parts of the property. However, problems can arise if any other owners do not meet their common property obligations and are under-insured. In the event of a claim for repairs to the common parts of the building, the cover provided by those who are not adequately insured may not be enough to pay the costs.

An alternative is a common insurance policy for the whole building, with each owner paying a share of the costs. Mortgage lenders will usually be willing to allow you to take out a share of a common policy rather than having your own insurance, provided the policy offers adequate cover. You will need to get a copy of the policy to show your lender.

If you buy a flat in a building that has a factor, you will probably find that there is already a common insurance policy covering the whole building. The duty to have this is usually in the title deeds. The factor collects each owner's share of the premiums and pays it to the insurance company. While you may object to having to pay towards a common policy, in many cases there is little you can do about it. Sometimes, the cover provided by a common policy has not been kept at an adequate level. This creates no problems if each owner has adequate cover but it can lead to problems if some owners are not adequately covered. If a common policy provided by a factor does not cover the reinstatement value of the building, you and your fellow owners can enforce the obligation in the courts.

3.13.5. Shared boundaries

Where you share a wall, be it part of a building or a boundary wall, fence or hedge that separates your property from another, you will probably have a joint responsibility for its maintenance. The title deeds may say what part is owned by whom and may specify the share of the maintenance. If the title deeds don't tell you, the boundaries and share of the maintenance will be determined by the Tenement Management Scheme (see 3.13.1).

3.14. Further information

Homestake: helping you to become a homeowner. Available from Homestake, Communities Scotland, Thistle House, 91 Haymarket Terrace, Edinburgh EH12 5HE. Tel: 0131 479 5269, email: homestake@communitiesscotland.gsi.gov.uk

http://www.communitiesscotland.gov.uk/stellent/groups/ public/documents/webpages/cs_008156.hcsp

Your right to buy your home. Available free of charge from the Scottish Executive, Victoria Quay, Edinburgh EH6 6QQ (tel: 0845 774 1741 or http://www.scotland.gov.uk/library5/housing/tbyh-00.asp), council housing departments and citizens' advice bureaux (see the phone book).

Rural Home Ownerships Grants. Contact Communities Scotland, Thistle House, 91 Haymarket Terrace, Edinburgh EH12 5HE (tel: 0131 313 0044).

Crofter Housing Grants and Loans. Contact Crofting Branch, Scottish Executive Environment and Rural Affairs Department, Room 106 Pentland House, 47 Robb's Loan, Edinburgh EH14 1TY (tel: 0131 244 6210) or your local SEERAD area office.

For information on the Lands Tribunal for Scotland, contact The Clerk to the Lands Tribunal for Scotland, 1 Grosvenor Crescent, Edinburgh EH12 5ER (tel: 0131 225 7996, e-mail: mailbox@lands-tribunal-scotland.org.uk, http://www.lands-tribunal-scotland.org.uk/).

Buying retirement housing. Factsheet 2S. Available free of charge from Age Concern, Freepost (SWB 30375), Ashburton, Devon TQ13 7ZZ (tel: 0800 00 99 66 or download from

http://www.ageconcernscotland.org.uk/pdf.pl?file=age/news/FS2sJUL05.pdf).

For details of the NHER and local assessors, contact the National Home Energy Rating Scheme, The National Energy Centre, Davy Avenue, Milton Keynes MK5 8NA (tel: 01908 672787, e-mail: enquiry@nesltd.co.uk, http://www.nher.co.uk/assessor-lists.shtml)

The following publications are available from the National House-Building Council Scotland, Suite 4, Pavilion 5, 5 New Mart Place, Edinburgh EH14 1RW (tel: 0870 850 4494, e-mail: cssupport@nhbc.co.uk, http://www.nhbc.co.uk):

NHBC – who we are, what we do.

Guide to your New Home

NHBC Buildmark. Your warranty and insurance cover.

The NHBC Sheltered Housing Code for builders and developers registered with NHBC. (Note that while the code covers Scotland, it is not compulsory here.)

Standards for conversion and renovations

Information on the Zurich Insurance Building Guarantee is available from Zurich Insurance Building Guarantee, 6 Southwood Crescent, Farnborough, Hampshire GU14 0NL (tel: 01252 377474, email: building.guarantee@uk.zurich.com, http://www.zurich.co.uk/buildingguarantee

Information on the Premier Guarantee is available from MD Insurance Services Limited, Haymarket Court, Hinson Street, Birkenhead CH41 5BX (tel: 0151 650 4343, e-mail: enquiries@ premierguarantee.co.uk, http://www.premierguarantee.co.uk/ index.htm)

Common Repair, Common Sense: a homeowner's guide to the management and maintenance of common property, is available free from solicitors, estate agents and HomePoint, Communities Scotland, Thistle House, 91 Haymarket Terrace, Edinburgh EH12 5HE (tel: 0131 313 0044, e-mail homepoint@communitiesscotland.gov. gsi.uk, download: http://www.homepoint.communitiesscotland. gov.uk/stellent/groups/public/documents/webpages/hmcs_ 006465.pdf)

Part 4

Buying a home: the legal process

4.1. Making an offer

Once you have decided which property you wish to buy, your solicitor or qualified conveyancer[1] (see 4.5.1) will need to make a formal written offer for it to the seller. The procedure for offering for a newly-built property is described in 4.4.

In Scotland, most houses and flats are sold through a system of 'blind bidding'. The seller asks for 'offers over' a particular price. This is an indication of the minimum price the seller expects to fetch. How much you will actually have to pay will depend very much on how busy the market is at that particular time and how much competition there is from other potential buyers. Some properties will be eagerly sought by many buyers because of their size or location. It will usually be possible to find out how much interest there is in a property by asking the seller how many people have noted interest in the property, or how many surveys have been carried out.

Sometimes property is advertised at a fixed price where the seller will accept the first offer for that amount. This may be because there is little activity in the market or the seller is looking for a quick sale. The seller may also offer the property at a fixed price as a starting point for negotiations on price. If you decide to make an offer, your solicitor will prepare one on your behalf and submit it to the seller's agent. If it is accepted without qualification, you will be in a legally binding contract, so it is essential that your loan arrangements are agreed beforehand.

---

[1] Further references to solicitors in this chapter apply equally to qualified conveyancers

The closing date

If a number of potential buyers show an interest in a property, the seller's agent will set a time and date – the closing date – for offers to be made. This should allow enough time for interested parties to arrange a valuation or survey (see Chapter 6) and finance for the purchase. If you are seriously considering making an offer, make sure your solicitor or qualified conveyancer formally notifies the seller's solicitor of your interest before you arrange a survey (see Chapter 6) and finance (see Chapter 5), or you may not be informed if a closing date is set. In some areas of Scotland, it is becoming more common for offers to be made subject to survey, in order to avoid the buyer paying for multiple surveys on properties they fail to buy.

You will have to decide how much you are prepared to, and can afford to, offer for the property, and then make your offer in competition with other potential buyers at the closing date. The seller does not have to accept the highest offer but usually will, unless it has unacceptable conditions attached. The seller may prefer an offer that has a later or earlier entry date if there is not much between the offers.

From 2008, potential purchasers must be provided with a survey report and other information about the property. Guidance on how the system will work will be available nearer the time.

If a closing date is not set, that may be because of a lack of interest in the property or simply a slow market and you may be able to negotiate a price for it.

4.2. The missives

Your offer to buy and the seller's acceptance must be made by your respective solicitors. They take the form of an exchange of letters known as missives.

Here are the sorts of things that will be in your offer, which your solicitor should explain to you. It should include a brief description of the property, the proposed date of entry and the price. It may also include any items, such as a cooker or carpets, which you wish to buy from the seller. It will also include a number of conditions, which vary from one transaction to another. For example, these are the main conditions you should expect:

- that there are no planning requirements or unreasonable conditions in the title deeds affecting the property;

- that planning and building control consents and completion certificates required for any alterations will be provided;

- that the street, pavement and main drains are public and maintained by the local authority;

- that there are no proposed road-widening schemes that may affect the property;

- that there are no outstanding statutory notices that affect the property, for example, a tree preservation order issued by the council;

- that the seller is genuinely the owner of the property and that his or her right to sell is not restricted in any way.

Your offer should ask the seller to accept it within a specified time. If you are buying a flat, your offer should also include conditions that the maintenance of the common parts is shared fairly, and that there are no outstanding charges for common repairs, for example for work to the roof agreed to by the seller (see the section on outstanding costs at 7.5).

The description

This could simply be the postal address, but if there is a garden, garage, or other outbuildings, then these should be specified in the offer.

The date of entry

This is the date on which you are to be given possession of the property, when you pay the seller the agreed price in exchange for a disposition (the legal document that transfers the title of the property from the seller to you). If you are relying on the proceeds of the sale of an existing property to help finance the purchase, you should try to get the dates to coincide. If you can't arrange this, you will have to take out a bridging loan to tide you over (see 5.6).

Concluding the missives

The seller may not accept some of your conditions and may wish to vary others, in which case he or she will return a 'qualified acceptance' of your offer. Your solicitor should explain what the terms of the qualified acceptance mean. Once the conditions and any qualifications are agreed, a formal letter of acceptance is sent and the missives are concluded. You will then have a binding contract.

4.3. Once the missives are concluded

Once you have an agreed contract with the seller, your solicitor will carry out the conveyancing. This is the legal process of transferring the title of the property from the seller to you. It is described in 4.5.

Mortgage and life insurance

If you are taking out a mortgage, you should make sure that an application has been made to the bank or building society and that any linked life insurance is in hand.

Buildings insurance

You should make sure that the property is adequately insured from the conclusion of the missives, although you are not legally required to do so until the date of entry, as the seller's insurance may not be adequate.

Title

It is possible for you and your spouse or partner to buy a home together by offering in both your names and having the title deeds prepared in your joint names. The deeds can provide that on the death of either of you, the title of that person shall pass automatically to the survivor. If you do this, it may affect any will made in the past or future, so you should discuss this with your solicitor.

4.4. Newly-built and newly-converted or renovated properties

The procedure for buying a newly-built home differs from buying an existing one. The home you see advertised may be part of an incomplete estate or may not even have been built yet, and it will usually be offered at a fixed price. Similarly, a conversion or renovation may be offered for sale before the work is complete. With a newly-built home, the builder makes an offer to sell to the buyer.

4.4.1. Newly-built property

Making an offer

Most builders have a standard form of offer that sets out the conditions on which they are prepared to sell. They will not usually vary these as they are designed to impose similar terms on all properties in a development. You should make sure that you have arranged your loan and taken legal advice before you accept the builder's offer, because your acceptance is legally binding. However, you may be able to reserve a home until you are ready to accept the offer by paying the builder a small deposit. It is at the builder's discretion whether to return the deposit if you do not go ahead, so ask before you pay it.

Deed of conditions

Normally, you will also be asked to accept, without adjustment, a deed of conditions. This sets out what you can and cannot do with your home, with the aim of protecting the appearance and use of the development. It may also provide for the setting up of a residents' association.

Stage payments

When you agree to buy a home that is not yet built, the builder may ask for stage payments. If you are buying with a mortgage, the lender will usually agree to release stage payments at certain stages. The stages depend on the type of construction and the lender's policy. The lender's surveyor will inspect each stage before payment, and you will have to pay the surveyor's fees. You should make sure that the stage payments in the builder's standard offer and the lender's mortgage offer coincide.

National House-Building Council Buildmark scheme

Buildmark is a 10 year warranty and protection scheme offered by NHBC-registered builders. It is not a guarantee. It protects you against the builder going bankrupt before the home is completed, provides an undertaking to repair faulty work within the first two years and insures against major damage of defined types and defects in the drainage for a further eight years.

Zurich Insurance Building Guarantee

This warranty is offered by builders registered with Zurich Insurance. From your acceptance of the builder's offer, it protects you against loss of money paid as a deposit in the event that the builder is unable to complete the contract due to liquidation, bankruptcy or fraud. It also provides ten years' cover against major structural damage and in year nine you can apply for an extension for a further five years. Acceptance will depend on the claims history. During the first two years of ownership, the builder is responsible for all damage and defects, as defined by the policy.

Premier Guarantee for New Homes

This guarantee is offered by builders registered with MD Insurance Services Limited. It protects you against loss of money paid as a deposit in the event that the builder is unable to complete the contract due to liquidation, bankruptcy or fraud, against defects for which the builder is responsible for two years and against major structural damage for a further eight years.

The NHBC scheme provides for arbitration by the Chartered Institute of Arbitrators of disputes that cannot be settled by conciliation. During the defects period, the Premier Guarantee provides for adjudication of disputes by the Royal Institution of Chartered Surveyors. If the builder does not accept the findings or fails to remedy the defect, the Premier Guarantee will meet the claim. As members of the Association of British Insurers, NHBC, Zurich Insurance and MD Insurance Services are bound by the ABI code of practice on complaints about insurance matters and complaints can also be made to the Financial Ombudsman Service. Details of the procedures for arbitration are available from the NHBC (see 3.14). There is no charge to complain to the ombudsman but arbitration might involve a fee and possible costs if you lose.

4.4.2. Newly-converted and renovated property

A home that has just been converted or renovated will not comply with the same building standards as a newly-built home. For example, the window frames in a new home are factory treated against wet rot, while in a conversion, if the frames are sound, a builder probably won't replace them. Also, a new home may be better soundproofed and insulated than a converted or renovated one. However, all of the work will have to comply with the Building Standards Regulations, which require much higher standards than you would find in an older home.

NHBC-registered builders may offer a conversion and renovations warranty if the work complies with the NHBC standards. This covers most aspects of the building and is aimed at ensuring that a sound job is done, rather than a superficial cosmetic exercise. The warranty obliges the builder to put right any defects reported during the first two years and provides insurance cover for builder bankruptcy either before the work is completed or during the first two years, and against major damage of defined types for the remainder of the 10 year period.

Zurich Insurance-registered builders may offer a warranty policy on conversions. While the cover is similar to that on newly-built homes (see 4.4.1), the builder's responsibility for defects is limited to the first year of ownership. It also protects against the loss of money paid as a deposit if the builder is unable to complete the contract due to liquidation, bankruptcy or fraud.

The Premier Guarantee offered on newly-built property by builders registered with MD Insurance Service Limited (see 4.4.1) may also be offered on newly-converted and renovated property.

4.5. Conveyancing

4.5.1. Introduction

Conveyancing is the process of transferring the title (ownership) of a property from the seller to the buyer. It starts as soon as the missives are concluded and you have a 'bargain', that is, a legally binding contract. Therefore, conveyancing is involved whether you are buying or selling or both. While it is theoretically possible to do the work yourself, conveyancing is a complex process that involves the most valuable asset you are likely to own. If you are taking out a mortgage, your lender will not, as a general rule, agree to you doing your own conveyancing. It is therefore safer to use a solicitor or a qualified conveyancer to do the work.

Traditionally, solicitors have carried out the legal work in buying and selling property. In addition, many offer an estate agency service or belong to a solicitors' property centre or both (see 7.2). You could also use a qualified conveyancer, who is not a solicitor but is qualified to carry out conveyancing. He or she must be registered with the Law Society of Scotland, which is responsible for setting standards for training and qualifications and for carrying out disciplinary functions. Most qualified conveyancers are employed by firms of solicitors. If you want to find an independent qualified conveyancer, you can get the names and addresses from the Law Society of Scotland or Registers of Scotland Executive Agency (see 4.10). Further references to solicitors in this chapter apply equally to qualified conveyancers.

A solicitor cannot act for two parties where his or her interests conflict or where there is a serious possibility that a conflict may arise, such as between a buyer and a seller.

You will be asked to sign documents at various stages of the process. Make sure that you are given an explanation of the meaning of any documents and that you understand them before you sign.

Unless you are a first-time buyer, the conveyancing involved in buying is usually carried out in parallel with the conveyancing involved in selling. If you are moving locally, your solicitor will carry out both procedures. However, if you are moving out of the area, you may find it more useful and convenient to use a local solicitor to do the conveyancing for your purchase.

Once you have a legally-binding contract, your solicitor will investigate the property and its title. Much of this is done by asking the seller's solicitor to provide any relevant information, supported by documents. Your solicitor will get the title deeds, including any deed of conditions that applies to the property, from the seller's solicitor and do the following.

- Check the land certificate and the deeds to make sure that the seller actually owns the property, and that the deeds are free from defects and do not contain any unusual or unreasonable conditions that will affect your use of the property.

- Tell you about any burdens (limitations or legal restrictions) or servitudes (obligations to allow someone to use the land or prevent you from making use of it) that affect the property.

- Check the rights of the 'superior' – a person or company who has retained some rights from the date of the property's original sale.

- Ask the local authority and water and sewerage authority whether there are any impending plans that might affect the property.

- Make sure that the ground burdens, such as factor's fees or maintenance charges for a common garden, are properly divided between you and the seller.

- Make a compensation payment to the former superior for feu duties, if applicable, where the date of entry is before 28 November 2006.

4.5.2. Standard security

This is the legal agreement that grants security over the property to your lender, if you have a mortgage. This means that if you don't keep up the loan repayments, the lender would be able to sell your home to recover the amount lent to you. The agreement has to be drawn up by a solicitor, and can normally be done by your solicitor, as long as your lender agrees to this. Although the work is being done for your lender, you are the one that pays for it, so it will be cheaper for you if your own solicitor can do it. So, check whether your lender will use your solicitor before instructing him or her. When the document is ready, you will have to sign it.

If you are married or in a civil partnership, and are buying the house in your name only, your solicitor must get your spouse's or civil partner's consent to grant the standard security to your lender.

4.5.3. Occupancy rights

When a husband and wife live together, but only one of them owns the home, the other has the right to live in it. Similarly, when a man and a woman are (or were) living together as if they were husband and wife, but only one of them owns the home and the other has been granted occupancy rights by a court, they have the right to live in it for the period granted by the court. From summer 2006, if two people in a civil partnership are living together, but only one of them owns the house, the other has the right to live in it. Your solicitor will check that there are no outstanding rights that could affect the transfer of ownership to you. If the seller is divorced or, from summer 2006, was in a civil partnership that was dissolved, your solicitor will check that no applications have been made to a court for a transfer of the property under the Family Law (Scotland) Act 1985.

4.5.4. The disposition

This is the legal document that transfers ownership of the property from the seller to you. Your solicitor drafts it and agrees its terms with the seller's solicitor. The seller will sign the document before the settlement so that the disposition, the deeds and the keys can be exchanged for your solicitor's cheque for the full purchase price on the date of entry.

4.5.5. Settlement

This is when you get possession of the property, and usually happens on the agreed date of entry. To do this, your solicitor will certify to your lender that the title is good; get the loan cheque from your lender; and obtain from you your contribution to the purchase price. In exchange for the cheque for the purchase price, your solicitor receives the disposition and other title documents, and the keys. The property is then yours. If you have a lender, it will retain the deeds as security over the property. If you don't have a lender you should ask your solicitor to keep them in safekeeping.

4.6. When you get the keys

Normally, the keys will be handed over as part of the settlement package in exchange for your solicitor's cheque for the full purchase price.

When you get the keys, there are a number of checks that you should make as soon as possible. You should check that all the items set out in the missives are there and that services, such as gas, electricity, water, and central heating are in working order. If anything is missing or not working, contact your solicitor immediately, or you may lose your contractual rights.

It is the seller's responsibility to take final readings of gas and electricity meters, but you should make a note of the readings when you get the keys so that you can check them against your first bills.

It may be difficult to check whether everything is working if the seller has not left operating instructions for the central heating system and other appliances. It's a good idea to go and see the seller in the run-up to the date of entry, and ask him or her to show you how to operate the central heating (and security system if there is one), where the electricity and gas meters are, and the stopcock to the water supply. If there are any appliances, such as a cooker or dishwasher, included in the sale, ask for any user's manuals or instruction booklets, and also for any guarantees or service agreements. However, remember that some agreements are not transferable.

If you are moving into a home that is newly-built or newly-converted by a member of the National House-Building Council, or one that is still covered by an NHBC warranty, make sure that you get a copy of the *Guide to your New Home* (see 3.14).

If you are moving into a home that is newly-built or newly-converted by a Zurich Insurance-registered builder, make sure you are given the insurance certificate, a copy of the policy document and the *Home Owner's Guide*. If a Zurich Insurance warranty is being transferred to you, make sure you notify Zurich Insurance of the change of ownership (see 3.14).

If you are moving into a home that is newly-built or newly-converted by a Premier Guarantee-registered builder, make sure you get the certificate of insurance and summary of the cover.

4.7. After settlement

4.7.1. Registration

After the settlement, your solicitor will register your ownership of the property and the standard security in favour of your lender in the Land Register of Scotland. The Land Register registers details of the current ownership, charges (securities or mortgages) over and burdens on properties. Its accuracy is guaranteed by the state.

4.7.2. Your title deeds

When your mortgage ends, your lender will offer to return your deeds. You will have to pay a fee for this. If you do not accept the offer, the lender can destroy your deeds, however historical. The Land Register entries are based on the title deeds and if an entry is later questioned, or it is alleged that a mistake has been made, it may be necessary to refer back to the original deeds. Therefore, it is unwise not to retain them. Although not all deeds and documents need to be kept, you should ask your solicitor for advice as to which are important to keep.

4.8. Costs

There are two elements to the costs: professional conveyancing fees and outlays. When you engage a solicitor, he or she must write to you at the earliest opportunity with an estimate of his or her total fee, including VAT and outlays, or the basis on which the fee will be charged. If you are buying and selling and using the same solicitor to do all the conveyancing, you may be offered a package deal on fees. Similarly, if you are using a solicitor to sell your property and do the conveyancing, you may be offered a package to cover the sale commission and conveyancing fees. If your mortgage lender is prepared to use your solicitor to prepare the standard security, as is normally the case, this will reduce your costs.

Conveyancing fees

A solicitor's fees and commission are not fixed but are open to negotiation, so you should shop around. The main factors he or she will take into account are the time involved in doing the work and the value of the property. The lowest fee is not a guarantee of the best service. If you choose a cheaper service, you may not get the same degree of personal service or the face-to-face advice that you may get elsewhere, so you should decide what is important to you. The fees should cover the following services:

- Preliminary work, including making the offer and exchanging missives, leading up to the conclusion of the bargain.

- Conveyancing.

- Handling the legal work connected with the loan part of the transaction.

As a general rule, a solicitor who has received money from you should put it in some sort of interest bearing account for you.

This, however, depends on the amount of money being held: smaller sums (less than £500), which should be paid out within two months, are not required to earn interest; larger sums, even for a short period, are.

Outlays

The costs outwith your solicitor's control are fees and taxes payable to the government, such as the fees due to Registers of Scotland, search fees and, where applicable, stamp duty land tax. The outlays that you will have to pay should be set out in the letter from your solicitor detailing the fees and outlays payable.

If you are taking out a loan, you will also have to pay for a mortgage valuation and, in some cases, an arrangement fee (see 5.5 for more information on this).

Registration fees

Fees are charged for applications for registration in the Land Register. The fees are based on the amount of money paid for a property. These range from £22 for a transaction of up to £10,000 to £7,500 for a transaction in excess of £5,000,000.

A standard security registered at the same time costs £22. If submitted separately, the fee ranges from £22 for a loan of up to £20,000 to £3,750 for a loan in excess of £5,000,000.

The fees are revised periodically and at the time of writing were under review. See 4.10 for where to obtain details of current fees.

Stamp duty land tax

This is a government tax on the purchase of a property that has to be paid where the price exceeds £125,000. The rate of duty is 1 per cent for prices of £125,001 to £250,000, 3 per cent for prices of £250,001 to £500,000 and 4 per cent for prices over £500,000. The tax is due on the full value, not just the excess over £125,000. If the property is in a disadvantaged area, the 1 per cent duty applies to prices from £150,001 to £250,000. See

4.10 for further information on these areas. If you are buying under the right to buy scheme (see 3.2), you pay duty on the discounted price, if applicable. You can save on the amount of duty to be paid if the purchase price includes items of furniture or appliances that can be distinguished from the price of the property.

When will payment be due?

You will normally be asked to pay for outlays such as those for advertisements, if you are selling, as and when they become due during the transaction, although most fees are usually paid at settlement. Where you are selling, your solicitor will normally deduct the fees and outlays from the proceeds of sale. Your solicitor is entitled to expect payment of his or her fees at settlement but you may be able to come to a different arrangement.

4.9. Complaints

Sometimes solicitors are negligent – they may do something that results in loss to the person who relied on their services. In other cases, their services may be unsatisfactory, inadequate or unprofessional. What you do depends on the type of complaint.

Professional services

You should let your solicitor know right away if you are unhappy with any aspect of his or her professional services. If you are unable to resolve the matter, take it up with the firm's client relations partner. Every solicitor's firm must have a written procedure for dealing with complaints. If you are still unable to resolve the matter, contact the Law Society of Scotland (see 4.10).

The Law Society has powers to deal with complaints about inadequate professional services or professional misconduct or both and excessive fees, and in appropriate cases can award compensation. In more serious cases of professional misconduct, not involving a claim of negligence, it will prosecute the solicitor before the Scottish Solicitors' Discipline Tribunal.

If you are dissatisfied about the handling of your complaint, you can complain to the Scottish Legal Services Ombudsman (see 4.10).

Negligence

Negligence may occur when a solicitor does not exercise a reasonable standard of skill and care and the client suffers a loss because of this, for example, by failing to register documents. If you consider that your solicitor has been negligent, you will need independent legal advice from a citizens' advice bureau or another solicitor if you wish to pursue such a claim. The Law Society of Scotland does not handle negligence claims.

The Law Society of Scotland maintains a list of solicitors who are prepared to advise on negligence claims against other solicitors (see 4.10).

There are proposals to establish a new independent body to deal with complaints against solicitors in Scotland. At the time of writing it was not clear what the proposals will be or when the new body will be established.

4.10. Further information

The following leaflets are available from Registers of Scotland Executive Agency:

The Edinburgh Customer Services Unit, Erskine House, 68 Queen Street, Edinburgh EH2 4NF (tel: 0845 607 0161) or Glasgow Customer Services Centre, 9 George Square, Glasgow G2 1DY (tel: 0845 607 0164). For both offices e-mail: customer.services @ros.gov.uk, http://www.ros.gov.uk/citizen/index.html:

Information available from Registers of Scotland

Registers of Scotland: a profile

Property searches, which includes a *Property search request form*

You can also get details of qualified conveyancers from the customer services centres or at http://www.ros.gov.uk/citizen/conveyancers.html

For information about the services provided by solicitors, details of local solicitors who do conveyancing work or independent qualified conveyancers, or about complaints procedures, contact the Law Society of Scotland, 26 Drumsheugh Gardens, Edinburgh EH3 7YR (tel: 0131 226 7411, client relations helpline: 0845 113 0018, e-mail: cro@lawscot.org.uk).

Details of postcodes qualifying for the stamp duty relief in disadvantaged areas can be found at http://www.hmrc.gov.uk/so/scotland.pdf or from the HM Revenue & Customs national advice service on tel: 0845 010 9000.

The Scottish Legal Services Ombudsman can be contacted at 17 Waterloo Place, Edinburgh EH1 3DL (tel: 0131 556 9123, e-mail: ombudsman@slso.org.uk, http://www.slso.org.uk/).

Part 5
Mortgages

5.1. Introduction

Most people buying a home need to take out a loan – a mortgage – to help pay for it. How much you need to borrow will depend on your personal circumstances, such as your financial situation and your age. A mortgage is likely to be your biggest and most important financial commitment, and it will be secured on your home. This means that the lender could sell your home if you don't keep up the loan repayments. So you need to be sure that you can afford the commitment or you will risk losing your home. You should also allow for the other costs involved in buying a home – valuation and survey fees, legal expenses, stamp duty land tax, registration fees and removal expenses.

Mortgages are available from a variety of lenders, such as building societies, banks, insurance companies, finance houses and specialist mortgage companies. If you are buying under your right to buy (see 3.2) and you have difficulty in arranging a mortgage, you can apply to your landlord for a loan.

When considering how much you can afford to borrow, and what type of loan would suit your circumstances, you may wish to get independent financial advice.

An independent financial adviser can advise on a range of financial products, such as insurance or investments, as opposed to a tied adviser who can only advise on one company's products. You should always shop around for advice. Financial advisers are regulated by the Financial Services Authority. You should check that any adviser you propose using is registered with the FSA and is independent. For more information, see 5.9.

These are some of the key questions you should ask of any prospective lender:

- Does the cost of the loan vary depending on whether you take out any linked purchases, such as buildings or life insurance?

- What are the costs and implications of transferring your mortgage from one lender to another? You should ask this of any existing and prospective lender.

- Can you use an endowment policy that you have for an existing endowment mortgage to cover a new endowment loan (see 5.3.2)?

- Can you use an existing life insurance policy as security for an individual savings account (ISA) mortgage (see 5.3.3) or personal pension plan mortgage (see 5.3.4)?

- What fees and costs are involved and what is the total amount payable?

5.2. How much can you borrow?

You should plan your finances at an early stage so that you do not over-commit yourself. Ask a potential lender how much it would allow you to borrow, but be warned that what a lender may lend you and what you can afford to borrow may not be the same. There are two factors a lender will consider: your income and the percentage of its valuation of the property that it would lend.

The amount you can borrow will usually be up to three times your gross annual earnings but may also take into account your other financial commitments. If you want a joint loan, it may be up to two and a half times your joint earnings.

The amount you can afford to borrow should take into account your current disposable income and how that may be affected in the future. For example, if you take out a joint loan based on your earnings and those of your partner or spouse, how will that be affected if you start a family and one of you takes time out of employment?

So, before you start to look for a home, you should find out, in principle, how much you could borrow. Don't forget that the lender's valuation may be less than the price you propose to pay and, if so, you will have to find the difference. For example, if you want to pay £160,000 for a property, which the lender values at £150,000 and it offers you an 80 per cent mortgage, that will be a mortgage of £120,000 (150,000 x 80% = 120,000). You will have to find the difference of £40,000, and all the other costs of the purchase.

If the property needs essential repairs to bring it up to the standard the lender requires, part of the mortgage may be withheld until you have carried them out.

5.3. Types of mortgages

A mortgage has two elements: the capital, which is the amount of money you borrow; and the interest, which is the money charged on the capital until you pay it back. There are different ways you can repay a mortgage. The main ways are as follows:

- *Repayment mortgage.* You make regular payments, usually monthly, of capital and interest.

- *Endowment or 'interest-only' mortgage.* You make regular payments of the interest only and repay the capital sum at the end of the mortgage term from the proceeds of an endowment policy to which you contribute during the term of the mortgage.

- *Individual savings account (ISA) mortgage:* You make regular payments of the interest only and repay the capital sum at the end of the mortgage term from the proceeds of an ISA to which you contribute during the term of the mortgage.

- *Personal pension plan mortgage.* You make regular payments of the interest only and repay the capital sum at the end of the mortgage term from the proceeds of a personal pension plan to which you contribute during the term of the mortgage.

You can always repay the loan before the end of the period for which it was arranged, although there may be an additional charge, especially if you do so within a few years of arranging it. You can pay off lump sums from time to time, or make regular overpayments if you have a 'flexible' mortgage, so reducing the period of payment. The shorter that period, the less your total interest bill.

5.3.1. Repayment mortgage

This is the simplest type of mortgage. You have one contract, with the lender, to whom you make regular repayments of capital and interest during the term of the loan. In the early years, these will be mainly interest but as the outstanding capital decreases, more of your payments go towards repaying the capital as the interest decreases.

The loan is usually paid off over 20 to 25 years. However, if you do not have as long as this before retiring, a lender may only offer you a shorter loan period.

5.3.2. Endowment or 'interest only' mortgage

With this type of mortgage, you have two contracts. The first is with the lender, to whom you repay only the interest over the period of the loan. The second is with a life insurance company with whom you take out an 'endowment life policy', which repays the capital at the end of the loan. You will be paying life insurance premiums and interest on the loan. If you die before the end of the loan period, the life policy will pay off the full debt.

The aim of a simple endowment mortgage is to provide you with the whole capital sum needed to pay off the loan at the end of the loan period, or before if you die. You can also take out a 'with profits' policy that may provide you with a lump sum in addition to the amount needed to pay off the loan. However, with any endowment policy, there is no guarantee of the capital value of the policy at the end of the mortgage period.

A 'with profits' endowment mortgage assumes that the eventual value of the policy will be greater than the sum assured, so that the initial sum assured can be lower than the amount of the loan. That reduces the premiums you pay and you may still receive an additional capital sum after you have paid off the loan. However, there is no guarantee of the eventual value of the endowment policy. If the value, with profits, is less than the amount of the loan, you will have to find the difference.

If you are considering an endowment mortgage, you should be very clear that there is a risk that the policy will not fully pay off the loan, and you must get independent financial advice (see 5.1).

5.3.3. Individual savings account mortgage

This is similar to an endowment mortgage in that you pay only the interest during the period of the loan. At the same time, you make regular payments into an individual savings account (ISA), and at the end of the mortgage period, you cash it in to pay off the full loan. There is currently a limit of £7,000 on the amount you can invest in an ISA in each tax year.

The value of ISAs depends on their value on the stock market, which can go down as well as up. Therefore, you run a risk that at the end of the mortgage period, your investment may not be worth enough to pay off the loan and you will have to find the difference. Because the ISA value is building up during the loan, a lender will probably require you to take out a life insurance policy for the amount of the mortgage in case you die before the end of the projected period of the loan. That makes this type of mortgage more expensive overall. However, if you are prepared to accept the risk, an ISA investment has the potential to do better than an endowment policy. An additional benefit of an ISA mortgage is that currently the proceeds of your investment are tax free.

Again, if you are considering one of these mortgages, it is important to get independent financial advice (see 5.1).

5.3.4. Personal pension plan mortgage

If you are self-employed and/or have a personal pension plan, you can link a mortgage to the pension plan. As with endowment and ISA mortgages, you pay only the interest during the period of the loan. At the same time, you make payments to a pension plan, which at the end of the loan period is designed to pay off the full loan and provide you with a pension.

You can only use the lump sum element of your pension plan to pay off the loan, and there is no guarantee that its value will be enough. If there is a shortfall, you will have to find the difference. This type of mortgage can offer substantial tax advantages. You can claim tax relief on your payments to the pension plan, and the lump sum you get when you retire is tax free.

You must get independent financial advice before considering this type of mortgage (see 5.1).

5.4. Interest rates

Whatever type of loan you choose, the interest rate is very important. All lenders will quote an annual percentage rate (APR), which is an approved system to help you compare the cost of the credit. The APR takes into account the added costs of a loan, such as arrangement fees, valuation fees and solicitor's charges. Generally, the higher the APR, the more expensive the credit. Some APRs will reflect short-term discounted or fixed rates, so you should check the monthly repayments and the sum paid over the whole term of the loan, and not just the initial APR.

While the general interest rates charged by lenders will be similar, many offer incentives for first-time buyers or to persuade you to switch to them, so you should shop around. Your solicitor or other independent adviser can help you. Some terms you may come across are as follows.

- *Variable rate.* Interest rates on deposits and mortgages vary according to the base rate (the rate, determined by banks, on which they base their lending rates of interest). Some lenders adjust the interest rate each time the base rate varies, others review your repayments annually, or you may be able to choose.

The variable rate is usually the lender's standard rate and it is generally worth looking at other options, as they may be cheaper.

- *Fixed rate.* The interest rate is set for a fixed period, for example, two, five or ten years and possibly even longer. This may help you to budget but it could be an expensive option if the general interest rate falls below the fixed rate. Unless the rate is fixed until the end of the mortgage, you are usually charged the lender's standard variable rate at the end of the fixed rate.

- *Capped-rate and collared-rate loans.* On a capped rate, the interest rate will not rise above an agreed maximum for a given period but will fall in line with the base rate. On a collared rate, the interest will not fall below an agreed minimum for a given period but will rise in line with the base rate. These may be combined in a cap and collar-rate loan. At the end of the period, you are usually charged the lender's standard variable rate.

- *Discounted-rate loans.* Many lenders offer new borrowers a discount of 1 per cent or more on the standard variable rate for a year or more.

- *Tracker mortgage.* The interest rate is a set amount above or below the Bank of England or some other base rate. It always tracks changes in that rate.

- *Deferred-interest loans.* These may be called 'low-start' mortgages. Parts of your repayments are deferred until a later time. The deferred interest is added to your loan so that the amount borrowed increases. At the end of the deferred period, there will be an increase, which may be substantial, in your monthly repayment. You will also have to agree to stay with the lender for a fixed period or face withdrawal penalties if you move to another lender.

- *Cash-back.* You will get a cash payment, usually between 3 per cent and 5 per cent, from the lender. The higher the cash payment, the greater and more complex are the number of strings likely to be attached. You may be faced with high redemption penalties over several years and you may also be offered a less competitive interest rate than is available elsewhere.

If you have a repayment mortgage on a variable interest rate and the interest rate increases, you may be able to extend the period of the loan, rather than increase your repayments.

5.5. Fees and penalties

Most lenders charge an arrangement fee for setting up capped, discounted, tracker or fixed-rate mortgages. This could be as much as £600, or more in some cases.

If you decide to change from a fixed, capped-rate, collared-rate, tracker or cash-back mortgage during the agreed period your lender is likely to make an early redemption charge, which can be from one to six months' interest. In addition, the lender may make a redemption charge if you change within a certain period after the agreed period. You may be better off staying in the scheme for the agreed period and then think about changing.

With a cash-back mortgage, the lender may require you to take out insurance through its agency, and the cash-back payment may affect your liability for Capital Gains Tax.

Some lenders may require a mortgage indemnity guarantee. They may also refer to it as a high percentage loan fee, high lending fee or additional security fee. This is a one-off premium, which is paid along with your first mortgage payment, that you pay to protect your lender (not you) if you fall significantly behind on your mortgage payments and it has to repossess your property and sell it. You may have to pay this if the value of your mortgage is above a threshold of 75 per cent to 80 per cent of the value of the property; this varies depending on the lender. For further information, see 5.9. The premium can be substantial – up to 8 per cent of the amount of the loan over the threshold – so you should check this when working out how much you can afford to borrow.

5.6. Bridging loans

If you are selling your present home and buying a new one, you may find that you have to produce the money to pay for your new home before you have received the proceeds from the sale of your old home. Banks and financial institutions will provide bridging loans to tide you over this gap.

You will not be able to take on a bridging loan before you have concluded the missives (see 7.5) on the sale of your present home. If you purchase your new home with a bridging loan, you will have to continue paying the mortgage on your present home as well as the interest on the bridging loan for your new home.

If you take out a bridging loan to tide you over between purchase and sale, the interest paid qualifies for tax relief at the basic rate.

5.7. Mortgage payment protection insurance

Your home is at risk if you do not keep up your mortgage payments. Mortgage payment protection policies will help you to pay your monthly mortgage and mortgage-related expenses if you become unemployed, disabled or unable to work. There is usually a waiting period, typically 30 to 60 days, before you can claim, after which the policy will normally cover your payments for up to one year. Policies will normally cover you against disability until you reach 65 and against unemployment until you reach retirement age or 65, whichever is earlier.

Mortgage payment protection insurance can be a valuable protection for your savings. If you have savings of over £8,000 you cannot get income support if you become unemployed. With savings of between £3,000 and £8,000 your income support will be affected. If you qualify for income support, you cannot get any income support to help with loan repayments for the first 39 weeks of unemployment or disability. Income support will only help with interest payments. It will not help with repayments of capital or with the premiums of any endowment or pension policy that is associated with the loan. The maximum qualifying loan is £100,000.

You should compare the different policies on offer, as the premiums and cover vary, depending particularly on your occupation. For example, you may not be eligible or cover may be limited if you are self-employed, a sole trader or a contract worker, or it may not cover both parties to a joint loan. If you are in one of those categories and are offered a policy, you should consider whether the limitations of the cover would provide you with any practical benefit. A mortgage payment protection policy will cost you between £3 and £9 a month per £100 of monthly payments you want to insure. You may be able to keep the costs down by opting for only one type of cover, for example, unemployment-only cover if your employer provides a high level of sick pay or if you have adequate permanent health insurance. It is strongly recommended that you read the terms of the insurance policy to be clear what is covered, what is excluded, and the amount of any excess.

Some insurance companies offer policies regardless of your lender, and some lenders have special offers of free cover for new borrowers, usually for a limited time. You should shop around to find the best policy for your needs. Many lenders are linked, or 'tied', to particular insurance companies. If you do not wish your choice to be limited in this way, you should get independent financial advice.

5.8. Life insurance

If you take out an endowment loan, the life insurance policy will pay off the full debt if you die before the end of the loan period. If you have a repayment loan, you should consider taking out a life insurance policy, which can be decreasing term insurance or level term insurance. The cover provided by a decreasing term policy decreases as the capital is repaid. The cover provided by a level term policy is equivalent to the amount of the original advance, irrespective of the actual loan debt. If you have an ISA or personal pension plan loan, the lender will probably require you to take out a level term life insurance policy.

However, while life insurance is of benefit to your lender and your dependants in assuring that your loan is repaid if you die, if you have no dependants, you should consider whether it is of any benefit to you. Also, if you take out a life policy in connection with an endowment or pension mortgage, this is likely to increase the amount of the loan fee.

For an initial sum insured of £100,000, a 30-year old non-smoker could expect to pay about £6 per month for a 25-year decreasing term policy or £7 per month for a 25-year level term policy.

5.9. Further information

The Financial Services Authority, 1 Canada Square, London E14 5AZ (consumer helpline: 0845 606 1234, minicom/textphone: 08457 300 104). The FSA does not deal with specific consumer complaints, recommend firms or give legal advice. However, the consumer helpline can answer general queries about financial products and services. It can also tell you if a firm is authorised and help 'sign post' you if you have a complaint and don't know who to contact. The following publications are available from the consumer helpline:

The world of mortgages laid bare, which can also be downloaded from

http://www.mortgageslaidbare.info/

Choosing the right mortgage – taking the right steps, an information pack of 12 leaflets, which can also be downloaded from

http://www.fsa.gov.uk/consumer/consumer_publications/mortgage_pack.html

You can also request hard copies of the information pack and other mortgage publications online from

http://www.fsa.gov.uk/consumer/consumer_publications/online/tpl_pubform.html

You can find further information on mortgage indemnity guarantees on the Council of Mortgage Lenders website: http://www.cml.org.uk/cml/consumers/guides/indemnity

The Association of British Insurers has guidance on *Payment Protection Insurance*, which is only available from its website at http://www.abi.org.uk/paymentprotectioninsurance

Part 6
Surveys and valuations

6.1. Introduction

When you find a home that you would like to buy, you and, if you are taking out a mortgage, your lender will want to have the property inspected to find out about its condition and its value. There are three basic types of inspection, each for a different purpose:

• Mortgage valuation (also known as a scheme 1 survey)

• Homebuyer's survey and valuation (also known as a scheme 2 survey)

• Building survey (also known as a structural survey)

How much you can expect to pay will depend on the type of inspection, with the building survey being the most expensive. While the fee may be based on the valuation figure, ask the lender or surveyor to tell you what the likely fee will be before the inspection is carried out.

From 2008, the seller or his or her agent will have to provide you with a survey report and other information about the property. Guidance on how the system will work will be available nearer the time.

6.2. Mortgage valuation report

A mortgage valuation report is *not* a survey. It is a limited report made for the benefit of building societies, banks and other lenders to guide them on the value of the property, to help them decide how much to lend. You have to pay for the inspection and although you may be given a copy of the report, you should not rely on it as a report on the condition of the building. If the surveyor or valuer is negligent, your legal rights may be less than if you had instructed the inspection yourself.

The inspection will be carried out by a valuer who is usually a qualified chartered surveyor. In this type of inspection, only major visible defects that affect the value of the property will be identified. The valuer will not inspect under floors, roof spaces and other parts that are not readily accessible, and the outside of the building and roof will be inspected from ground level only.

If defects are identified, the valuer may recommend that the lender keeps part of the loan until you have carried out certain repairs. The valuer may also recommend that you commission a more extensive specialist survey, if it is suspected that there may be something wrong which may affect the value of the property. If you decide to do this, you should also get an estimate for the cost of any repairs, and take these costs into account when deciding how much to offer or whether to offer at all.

6.3. Homebuyer's survey and valuation

This kind of survey is different from a mortgage valuation report, in that it is you who instructs the surveyor, who will have a direct responsibility to you to carry out the work with reasonable care and skill. If the surveyor is negligent, and you suffer loss as a result, you may be able to take legal action. Your solicitor should be able to give you guidance about which surveyor to choose, and it's a good idea to find out beforehand whether your lender will accept the surveyor's report, which will contain an opinion about the value of the property, for lending purposes.

The Royal Institution of Chartered Surveyors in Scotland produces a standard report form that can be used for houses and flats. However, if you or the surveyor feels that the standard form is not suitable, you can commission a private survey, which allows more flexibility for the surveyor. The survey will cover the same things, regardless of the form it is in. You should be clear about what the survey will cover before the surveyor visits the property and get this confirmed in writing.

The survey will cover the outside of the property, such as the general condition of the woodwork, gutters and downpipes, dampness in walls, damp-proofing, insulation, drainage and under-floor ventilation. If there is no ready access to the roof, under floors or to cellar space, inside or outside, these will not be given a detailed inspection but you should be told about this in the report. Inside, the condition of services, such as wiring, drainage and central heating will be commented on but the surveyor will not check to see if they are working properly. The report will include the estimated cost of rebuilding the property for buildings insurance purposes and the value of the property on the open market.

Although this type of survey should contain the information you need to assess the property, the detail will depend on what the seller will allow the surveyor to do. The surveyor will not be able to comment on parts of the property that can't be reached or seen, such as under fitted carpets. However, the surveyor may recommend further investigations that can only be made by lifting carpets, for example, to look for dry rot. In this case, you should commission a specialist survey and get estimates for the cost of any work before you make an offer. This can only be carried out if the seller will allow suitable access.

This type of survey is likely to cost at least twice as much as a mortgage valuation inspection, but you will get much more information. If you consider the cost of putting things right that were unforeseen, it may well be a price worth paying.

Some firms offer the option of hidden defects insurance when they carry out a homebuyer's survey and valuation. This may carry an extra cost and its availability will vary from firm to firm. If this is of interest to you, it is worth checking before you instruct your survey. The insurance covers the cost of repairing expensive defects that were not seen and reported on at the time of inspection because they were concealed or inaccessible due to carpets, furniture or wall coverings, and so on. The twelve-month policy covers claims up to £100,000 subject to the exclusion of the first £500 of any claim. You should check the terms of the insurance policy against the survey report before deciding whether it is worth the extra cost.

6.4. Building survey

This type of survey is a detailed examination of the whole property and its services and is carried out by a chartered building surveyor. It is rarely used in Scotland, partly because of the speed at which home purchase normally takes place and because most sellers are unlikely to allow such a survey unless there is a very limited market for the property and you have expressed a very strong interest. However, if you are thinking of buying a very old or unusual type of property, a property you plan to renovate or alter, or a property that has had extensive alterations, a building survey may be advisable.

The survey is very detailed and could mean some disturbance to the property, such as sawing into timbers to check for rot or drilling into walls to check for dampness. The survey may include or recommend specialist inspection of the drainage, electrical system, central heating and timbers. There may still be some restrictions on access to covered floors and roof spaces but, within these restrictions, the survey will be complete.

Because of the work required for the report, this type of inspection will cost considerably more than any other. The cost may be further increased if tradesmen are brought in to do any work. You should ask the surveyor to tell you the likely price before instructing the survey. If you want the report to include a valuation, you should ask for this when you commission the survey.

6.5. Insurance

All types of survey report will normally recommend the approximate level of insurance required to cover reinstatement of the property. Your lender will require you to have buildings insurance, and the reinstatement cost is the estimate of how much it would cost to rebuild the property should it be destroyed, for instance by fire. Where appropriate, it will include outbuilding and garages, demolition and site clearance and certain professional fees.

While it will reflect the surveyor's local knowledge and available statistical building cost information, it is not a definitive statement of the exact costs of reconstruction and is provided only for general guidance.

6.6. Complaints about chartered surveyors

It is important to take care when deciding which survey would best suit your needs, and to be clear about what each kind of survey will and will not provide. Sometimes buyers arrange a basic mortgage valuation inspection and are disappointed when they don't get as much information as they expected. However, sometimes surveyors are negligent: they may miss something about the property that was important which results in loss to the person who relied on the survey. In these circumstances, it may be necessary to take legal action. In other cases, a surveyor's conduct may be unsatisfactory or unprofessional and, in these circumstances, you can complain to the surveyor's firm, his or her professional body or to the surveyor ombudsman.

Only members of the Royal Institution of Chartered Surveyors (RICS) can call themselves 'a chartered surveyor'. They will have the initials TechRICS, MRICS or FRICS after their names.

If you have a complaint about a firm of chartered surveyors (or one where at least one partner is a chartered surveyor), you should first try to resolve it through the firm's complaints handling procedure. All chartered surveyors' firms must have one and details of how to use it should be included in any correspondence to you. If it is not resolved, you should write to the Professional Conduct Department at the RICS (see 6.7). Your letter should contain permission for the RICS to send a copy of your complaint and any documents to the firm involved.

The RICS can only investigate complaints alleging professional misconduct, including:

• unjustifiable delay in dealing with your affairs;

• failure to reply to letters;

• disclosure of confidential information;

• failure to disclose a conflict of interest;

- failure to look after your money. RICS members must keep your money in a separate 'client account' and maintain a record of all transactions.

A conflict of interest may arise if your interests conflict with the private interests of the surveyor or with the interests of another client. The surveyor must tell you this in writing. You must also be told that this firm cannot act for you until you get separate independent professional advice.

A chartered surveyor who is found to have breached the RICS by-laws or code of conduct can be reprimanded, suspended or expelled from membership. The RICS will not comment on, or investigate, cases where you have a remedy in law, nor will it assess or award compensation. In cases such as alleged professional negligence or breach of contract, or where you believe that you have a claim for compensation, you should consult a citizens' advice bureau (see the phone book) or a solicitor.

Surveyor ombudsman scheme

The surveyor ombudsman offers a free and independent review of consumer complaints about surveying services provided by chartered surveyors in Scotland who are members of the RICS. The ombudsman will only consider a complaint that has not been resolved by the surveyor concerned. The ombudsman can investigate:

- possible breaches of a chartered surveyor's legal obligations;

- unfair treatment;

- financial loss or maladministration.

That might include avoidable delay, failure to follow proper procedures, rudeness or discourtesy, not explaining matters, refusing to deal with a complaint fully or promptly, poor service and incompetence. The ombudsman can award compensation for loss or expenses of up to £25,000 or for stress and inconvenience of up to £500. For further information, see 6.7.

Arbitration

You could also use the Surveyors' Arbitration Scheme or take the firm to court. The arbitration scheme is designed to resolve disputes cheaply and quickly. It is independently administered by the Chartered Institute of Arbitrators (see 6.7). While less formal than a court, the decision is legally binding. Before you can use the arbitration scheme, you must first try to resolve your complaint through the firm's in-house complaints handling procedure. All RICS members must agree to arbitration.

6.7. Further information

A directory of chartered surveyors in Scotland and guides to understanding property surveys, and home buying and selling are available free of charge from the RICS contact centre: tel: 0870 333 1600, e-mail: contactrics@rics.org. Ask for information on services in Scotland. You can also get informal advice from the professional information team at the contact centre.

Complaints about chartered surveyors should be addressed to the Director, The Royal Institution of Chartered Surveyors in Scotland, 9 Manor Place, Edinburgh EH3 7DN (tel: 0131 225 7078, e-mail: contactrics@rics.org.uk)

Information on the Surveyor Ombudsman Scheme is available from the Surveyor Ombudsman Scheme, PO Box 21537, Stirling FK8 3YD (tel: 01786 860715, e-mail: enquiries@surveyor ombudsman.org.uk, http://www.surveyorombudsman.org.uk/

For more information about the Surveyors Arbitration Scheme, contact The Chartered Institute of Arbitrators, Dispute Resolution Services, International Arbitration and Mediation Centre, 12 Bloomsbury Square, London WC1A 2LP (tel: 020 7421 7444, e-mail: info@arbitrators.org).

Part 7

Selling your home

7.1. Introduction

If you are selling your home and buying another in Scotland, you should also read Chapters 3 and 4. This chapter concentrates on the procedures not covered in those chapters.

As soon as you decide to sell your home, you should tell your solicitor so that he or she can retrieve your title deeds from your lender. This is so that they can be checked and be available for the buyer's solicitor to view. You should also tell him or her about any alterations, extensions or treatments you have done and check that all the necessary documents are available. You should also check with your lender how much money is needed to pay off the loan on the property.

There are a number of things you should do before putting your home on the market.

• You should discuss your plans with a solicitor or qualified conveyancer (see 4.5.1). Even if you plan to do your own advertising and marketing, it is not usually practicable to do the legal work yourself (see 7.5). Your solicitor will retrieve the title deeds from your lender (if you have a loan) and check that you have a good title to the property (see 4.5.1). He or she will also initiate local authority searches to make sure that there are no outstanding notices, orders or proposals affecting the property.

• If you own your home jointly with one or more others, you must get their consent before you can sell. If you are married, and your spouse is not a co-owner, the Matrimonial Homes (Family Protection) (Scotland) Act 1981 requires that you get his or her consent for the sale. Similarly, from summer 2006, if you are in a civil partnership, and your partner is not a co-owner, the Civil Partnership Act 2004 requires that you get his or her consent for the sale. Without this consent, you cannot give a purchaser possession of the property. This is particularly important if you are separated from your spouse or civil partner.

From 2008, you or your agent will have to provide potential purchasers with a survey report and other information about the property. Guidance on how the system will work will be available nearer the time. You will not have to provide this information if you are selling to a member of your family.

Here are some things you might wish to consider before you put your home on the market.

• Is it worth doing any repairs or redecorating? Beyond carrying out necessary repairs, don't redecorate unless the home badly needs it. Anyone buying your home may wish to redecorate it to his or her own taste. If you do redecorate, keep to pale, neutral colours.

• Make sure that everything is in working order and that the home is thoroughly cleaned. In particular, if you have central heating, it is worth having your boiler serviced if you do not already have a service plan. If you have a garden, make sure that it is tidy and the grass is cut before people come to view.

• If you have made any changes that required planning permission or building control consent, check that you have the necessary documents and that your solicitor is aware of these. If you have made changes that required permission but you failed to get it at the time, it may be possible to get retrospective permission. Otherwise, you will have difficulty in selling your home. You can check whether you need permission and how to get this by contacting the planning or building control department at your local council.

• If you have had any remedial treatment carried out, for example, for wet or dry rot, or installed a damp-proof course that is covered by a guarantee or insurance, check that the certificates or policies are available and valid, and that the company providing

them is still in business. You will also need a description of the
work done, such as the original estimate.

7.2. Advertising and marketing your home

You can advertise and market your home yourself or use an
agent, such as an estate agent or solicitor. Many solicitors provide
a full estate agency service.

7.2.1. Doing it yourself

Doing your own advertising and marketing will save you an
agent's commission but you will have to spend some money on
advertising and put your own time into it. From 2008, if you do
your own marketing, you will have to provide a survey report
and other information about the property to potential buyers.
Guidance on how the system will work will be available nearer
the time.

How much should you ask for? There are a number of ways to
decide on an asking price.

• Consider how much you paid for the home, as a possible starting
  point, but bear in mind that increases in home prices have varied
  considerably in different parts of the country in recent years.

• Look at the asking prices for similar properties in your area
  advertised in estate agents' windows and in newspaper
  advertisements. If you live on a modern estate where houses
  similar to yours are up for sale, it will be easier to work out a
  price than if you live in an older or more individual home.

• Look at the house price guides provided as supplements with
  some newspapers and available on the internet, for example,
  http://www.scotlandshouseprices.gov.uk, which give details of
  the sale price of similar homes sold in your area.

• Ask your solicitor. He or she may have knowledge of the local
  market and be able to advise you.

• Ask an estate agent for a valuation. Make it clear that you are not
  asking the agent to sell your home. You will probably have to

pay a valuation fee, although in areas where there is competition between agents, you may be offered a free valuation.

• Ask a chartered surveyor to do a survey and valuation. You will have to pay a fee but if you have lived in your home for many years, this is a useful way of identifying any problems that you should take into account in setting your asking price. Also, you will not be taken by surprise if a potential buyer's surveyor discovers them.

Some newsagents and supermarkets have notice boards where you can put up a card. Your employer may have one. You can advertise in the local or national (Scottish) press and on property websites. Use the descriptions given in the property pages as a guide to describing your own home.

Prepare a typewritten property description sheet to hand out to viewers. For guidance, visit some estate agents and collect property description sheets for properties similar to yours. Avoid flowery language and describe the property accurately and truthfully.

From 2008, if you do your own marketing, you will have to compile a purchaser's information pack. Guidance on how the system will work will be available nearer the time

Decide what you want to include in the asking price. For example, carpets, curtains, appliances and furniture that you don't want to take with you could be included, or listed separately at a fixed price or at a price to be negotiated.

Your property description should include the name, address and phone number of your solicitor to whom expressions of interest and formal written offers should be made. Give details of times and days that surveyors or valuers can call. Send a copy of the property description to your solicitor.

A 'For Sale' sign is useful for alerting people who may be looking around your area for properties for sale and it will help people who have already contacted you to find you. To avoid being pestered by people calling without an appointment, put your phone number on the sign and 'By appointment only'.

7.2.2. Using an agent

There are advantages in using an agent, who could be an estate agent or a solicitor:

• they have experience of the local market, and can advise on the potential value of your home;

• they can advertise and market your home more extensively than you can;

• they are likely to have a bank of potential buyers prior to marketing;

• they can arrange a mortgage for a potential buyer, if necessary;

• if you are elderly or live alone, or don't have the time, you can ask them to accompany viewers.

By law, estate agents must:

• give you their terms in writing and say whether they are acting as a multi, joint or sole agent;

• explain their fees;

• declare any personal or connected interests;

• report any offers (unless the seller instructs otherwise) in writing quickly;

• have separate accounts for clients' money;

• not misrepresent any offers.

An agent will prepare the property description for your home, advise you on the potential selling price and asking price, advertise and market it for sale, deal with enquiries and advise you on offers. From 2008, your agent will also be responsible for providing additional information on the property. Guidance on how the system will work will be available nearer the time.

If you use an estate agent, you can give sole agency rights to one agent or instruct as many as you wish. The commission is usually about 1.5 per cent of the selling price, although with sole agency rights, you may be able to negotiate a lower commission. You should shop around. Ask for a written estimate of the total charges, including commission, advertising and VAT. The agent will send any formal offers to your solicitor.

If you use an estate agent, it is a good idea to find one who is a member of the National Association of Estate Agents or the Ombudsman for Estate Agents scheme. Estate agents who are members of these bodies are bound by strict rules of conduct (NAEA members) or a code of practice (OEA members) (see 7.6). This means that if you complain and the agent does not deal with this to your satisfaction, you can contact the organisation overseeing it and it will investigate the matter further. See 7.7 for how to get a list of member agents in your area. Similarly, solicitors are bound by the code of conduct and disciplinary rules of the Law Society of Scotland (see 4.9).

A solicitor will either advertise and market your property himself or herself or register it with a local solicitors' property centre. The centre will charge a fee to cover display of the property details and an insert in its property listing, mailing list or website. The solicitor will charge a commission of about 1.5 per cent of the selling price in addition to the conveyancing fees. Some solicitors may charge a lower commission or offer a package to cover selling and conveyancing for your sale and also your purchase, so you should shop around and ask for estimates. Once you have engaged a solicitor, he or she must write to you at the earliest opportunity with an estimate of the total fee, including VAT and outlays, or the basis on which the fee will be charged.

7.3. Fixing a closing date

The closing date is the time and date by which formal written offers must be submitted to your solicitor. If you use an estate agent, the offers will usually be sent to them.

Whether you fix a closing date depends on the amount of activity in the housing market and the level of interest in your property. If there is little interest, or the market is very quiet, you will have to decide how long to wait for expressions of interest to accumulate or whether to let it be known that you will consider an individual offer. If you wait too long, potential buyers may find another property. You should get guidance from your agent on this.

You should only fix a closing date when several people have made formal expressions of interest to your solicitor. If someone instructs a valuation or survey or both, that is a good indication of serious interest, but it is by no means certain that an offer will necessarily follow. Increasingly, buyers may offer 'subject to survey' to avoid spending money on multiple survey fees for properties they then do not succeed in buying. You should resist offers for a quick sale if there are several people interested in buying.

7.4. Accepting an offer and concluding the missives

You do not have to accept the highest offer made at the closing date, or indeed any offer at all. Usually, the offer will include a number of conditions to suit the person making the offer. These include the date of entry, and any items to be included in the price, such as carpets and curtains, and technical conditions about, for example, planning permission, building control consent, guarantees and warranties.

It is up to you to decide which offer you want to accept. While usually you will want to accept the highest offer, other conditions, such as the date of entry, may also be important you. If the highest offer comes with conditions you don't want to accept, then your solicitor will find out whether there is any room for negotiation. For example, if the highest offer is subject to survey, you will have to decide whether to accept that offer and risk losing other potential buyers, and also risk the buyer reducing his or her offer or withdrawing it because of an adverse survey report. If you are not happy with the conditions, you will then have to decide whether to accept the next highest offer. You could also decide not to accept any of the offers, and re-advertise.

Your agent, if you have one, will normally deal with the main conditions in the offer including the price, the date of entry and the extras that will be included in the sale (such as carpets and curtains). They may negotiate on your behalf to try and change the date of entry and inclusions. If the property is sold at a closing date they will not be able to negotiate on the sale price.

Once you have made a decision, the offer will be passed on to your solicitor (if he or she is not also your agent) who will discuss the offer terms with you in more detail before issuing a letter known as a qualified acceptance, which sets out your acceptance of the offer, subject to those conditions that need to be changed.

Usually, there will then be an exchange of letters (missives) in which your solicitor will try to vary any unacceptable conditions. Normally, this only takes a few days, but sometimes takes longer if there are any unusual conditions in either the offer or qualified acceptance. Once both sides agree, the missives are concluded, and at that stage there is a binding agreement between you. Until the missives are concluded, either party can withdraw without penalty.

7.5. Once the missives are concluded

Once the missives are concluded, your solicitor will do the conveyancing, which is the legal transfer of the title from you to the buyer. The procedures for doing the conveyancing for a sale are similar to those for a purchase (see 4.5) but from a different perspective. They mainly involve your solicitor responding to the buyer's solicitor's enquiries. Your solicitor will also agree the disposition drafted by the buyer's solicitor, arrange for the repayment and discharge of your loan over the property, and redeem your feu duty if necessary. Just before the settlement, you should sign the disposition and make arrangements to hand over the keys.

After the settlement, your solicitor will settle your mortgage account and pay the balance to you after deducting his or her fees and expenses, or put the balance towards the purchase of your new home if you are also buying.

Information on conveyancing fees is given under costs in 4.8. When you are selling, the fees should cover:

• Preliminary work, including exchanging missives, leading up to the conclusion of the bargain.

• Conveyancing.

• Handling the legal work connected with the discharge of the loan.

While this is being done, there are a number of things for you to attend to. They are described below and in Chapter 8.

Insurance and maintenance

Although the risk of loss or damage to the property passes to the buyer when missives are concluded, you should keep your own building and contents insurance in force until the date of entry, because you are responsible for maintaining the property until then. Sometimes the buyer will ask to visit the home before the date of entry, perhaps to measure up for curtains. While this is perfectly all right, it would not be a good idea to allow the buyer to do any significant work on the home before the date of entry, such as installing a cooker. There is always a chance that something may go wrong. Make sure that you tell your solicitor if you arrange for any repairs or find out about any local authority notices that affect the property.

Outstanding costs

If you live in a flat and you are liable for any costs incurred as a result of a decision made under the terms of your title deeds or the Tenement Management Scheme, you will remain liable if the work or maintenance is arranged or carried out before the date your flat changes hands. However, before you sell, you, your fellow owners or your property manager can register a notice in the Land Register of Scotland or the Register of Sasines, depending on where your title deeds are registered, that you are potentially liable for unpaid costs. If a notice is registered at least 14 days before the date that the new owner acquires ownership, then your liability will be shared with the new owner (see *Common Repair, Common Sense* at 3.14).

Hire purchase, credit agreements and loans

Your contract with the buyer will normally require that there are no hire purchase or credit agreements or home improvement loans outstanding on any items included in the sale on the date of entry. Make sure that any of these are paid off before the date of entry.

Periodic charges and outgoings

If you are paying any communal or factor's charges, you should give your solicitor details of these so that they can be apportioned at the date of entry. You should also make sure that he or she has details of your council tax banding and pay all outstanding charges until the date of entry.

Settlement

At settlement, a disposition (the legal document transferring the ownership or title from you to the buyer) in favour of the buyer is exchanged for the buyer's solicitor's cheque for the full purchase price. Your solicitor will pay any outstanding loans on the property from the sale proceeds, take off his or her fees and outgoings, and either give you a cheque for what is left, or put this towards the purchase price for your new home. You should also be given a detailed statement of all the transactions. Normally, you will receive the statement and any cheque on the day the sale is completed or very shortly afterwards.

The keys

Arrange with your solicitor to hand over the keys to the buyer. You can either deliver them to your solicitor on the date of entry or ask him or her to contact you and tell you when you can hand them over. **Never** hand over the keys before this.

7.6. Complaints

Complaints about solicitors are covered at 4.9.

If you are unhappy with your estate agent's services, you should first try to sort things out directly with the estate agent.

If you are still not happy, you can complain to either the National Association of Estate Agents, if the agent is a member, or to the Ombudsman for Estate Agents, if the agent is a member of the ombudsman scheme. However, estate agents are not required to belong to either of these schemes. Even if they are not, you may be able to complain to your local trading standards department where there is an alleged breach of the Estate Agents Act or the Property Misdescriptions Act. You can find guidance on the latter Act on the Department of Trade and Industry's website at http://www.dti.gov.uk/ccp/topics1/guide/property_description.htm

National Association of Estate Agents members

Estate agents who are members of the National Association of Estate Agents have the letters ANAEA, MNAEA or FMAEA after their names and the NAEA logo on their premises and stationery. Members of the association are required to comply with the Rules of Conduct and Code of Practice for Residential Estate Agency, which includes having an internal complaints procedure and a designated senior member of staff to deal with complaints.

If you have a complaint about an estate agent, you should first complain to the agent to attempt to resolve the problem. If you are unable to resolve your complaint, you should complain to the NAEA compliance officer (see 7.7). The Association will look into all complaints providing there is no alternative means of resolving them. The Association will not deal with complaints involving:

• Money outstanding or compensation, which you can take to the small claims court. You should get independent legal advice from a citizens' advice bureau or a solicitor before doing so.

• Allegations of a breach of the Estate Agents Act 1979 or the Property Misdescriptions Act 1991, which you should refer to the trading standards department of your local council.

- Matters on which legal proceedings have been started until the proceedings have been concluded.

- Conduct that occurred more than two years before you complained.

The Association can discipline members found to be in breach of the rules of conduct and code of practice by a caution or formal warning. Members can also be brought before a disciplinary tribunal, which has the power to fine them for each breach of the rules, or to suspend or expel them from membership.

Ombudsman for Estate Agents members

If you are unable to resolve a complaint with a member of the NAEA through the NAEA's complaints procedure, or if the agent is not a member of the NAEA, you should find out if the agent is a member of the Ombudsman for Estate Agents scheme (see 7.7). The Ombudsman for Estate Agents will attempt to resolve complaints against members of the scheme by mediation or conciliation. If that fails and the ombudsman supports your complaint, the ombudsman has the power to award you compensation, which is binding on the agent.

7.7. Further information

The National Association of Estate Agents can be contacted at: Arbon House, 21 Jury Street, Warwick CV34 4EH (tel: 01926 496800, e-mail: info@naea.co.uk) or visit the NAEA website http://www.naea.co.uk/agents/default.asp to find local members. To make a complaint about a member, write to the Compliance Officer at the above address, or e-mail: compliance@naea.co.uk

To make a complaint about a member of the Ombudsman for Estate Agents scheme, contact The Ombudsman for Estate Agents, Beckett House, 4 Bridge Street, Salisbury, Wiltshire SP1 2LX (tel: 01722 333306). You can find information about the scheme and a list of members at http://www.oea.co.uk/complaints/complaint.htm

Part 8

Organising the move

8.1. Doing it yourself or using a removal company

Doing your own move with the help of family or friends is a lot less expensive than using a removal company. Whether it is practical for you to do-it-yourself will depend on:

• the amount of furniture and other possessions you have;

• whether you can handle large or awkward items of furniture;

• the ease of exit from your current home and entry to your new home;

• the availability of willing and able helpers;

• whether you are fit and strong enough;

• whether you have other commitments, for example, children or work, which cut down the time you have available to get organised;

• the distance involved.

The basic cost of doing-it-yourself is the van hire charge, insurance to cover the move and petrol, or insurance and petrol alone if you can borrow a van from a friend or your employer. Before you hire or borrow a van, be sure that you can cope with driving it and that it is big enough to avoid making too many trips. There is a limit of 7.5 tonnes laden weight to a van you can drive with an ordinary licence from the age of 18. Hire firms can set their own minimum age limits above this and will usually require you to have held a full, clean licence for at least one year.

The more you have to move and the further the distance, the more sense it makes to use a removal company.

8.2. Finding a remover and getting a quotation

Get a quotation from two or three removal companies. If you have used a removal company before and were happy with its service, ask it to quote. You can find other companies through personal recommendation, in the *Yellow Pages* or on the internet. The British Association of Removers (BAR) is the trade organisation that represents most leading removal and storage companies. For the names of some of its local members, contact the BAR (see 8.8). A smaller trade organisation is the National Guild of Removers and Storers (NGRS). For the names of some of its local members, contact the NGRS (see 8.8).

When the estimators come round, remember to show them what you have to move in the garage, garden and loft, as well as your home contents. Decide whether to do your own packing or to ask the removers to do this, so that you can compare quotes. Assess the value of your home, what needs special attention (such as certain pieces of furniture or clothes) and discuss this with the estimator. Packing some items yourself may save you some money but the removers will not accept responsibility for items they did not pack.

If you want to put your home contents into store, most removal companies will charge a weekly rate according to the volume, with a minimum storage charge of four weeks. Make sure you ask the contractor for 'keep forward' labels to attach to any items you may want in advance of complete clearance.

Removers will unpack for you, if this was included in the quotation. This could be important if you work full-time, are elderly, unfit or have small children. However, it will be more expensive and you will need to decide in advance where everything is to go.

Most removal companies will sell you packaging materials and will lend you cartons for linen, pictures/mirrors, books and china, and temporary wardrobes for clothes.

You are responsible for arranging the disconnection of electric light fittings, appliances and mains services such as gas and telephone. It is also your responsibility to tell the remover about access to your new home, for example, whether there is a lift, problems with parking, a long driveway or narrow staircases to be negotiated.

Removal costs take account of the time taken, the distance to be travelled and the volume of your possessions. A company may charge you more if you have possessions that are particularly heavy or difficult to move, for example, a piano or large, heavy wardrobe. Quotations for your removal will vary according to the companies' workloads, the time of year and day of the week. Fridays and the beginning and end of the month are always the busiest times. Choosing a different day of the week and time of the month could save you as much as 20 per cent.

The lowest quotation is not necessarily the best. You are moving your home, so check carefully what is included and what is excluded in the services offered.

8.3. Insurance

If you have a home contents insurance policy, it may cover your possessions during a move. If not, you may be able to get a temporary extension, for an additional premium. An insurance company is unlikely to offer you insurance for a move if you do not already have a policy with it. Most removal companies and all BAR and NGRS members provide a minimum level of insurance. BAR members are bound by BAR's liability terms, which require that they are insured. Once you have declared the total value of your goods, the remover accepts liability for them. Normally, liability is set at £25,000, although you can increase the value at an additional cost.

Whether you rely on your own insurance or the remover's insurance, check that the cover offered is appropriate and adequate and make a note of the time limit for claims. Don't forget that the remover's insurance will not cover items you pack yourself. If you rely on your own home contents insurance for cover, it may also exclude items you pack yourself. Check with your insurance company.

8.4. Planning your move

Plan ahead. There is a checklist at 8.6, which includes the information below.

The date. Arrange this as far ahead as possible. Cancellation or postponement can be costly.

Your new home. A map showing your new address and a contact telephone number will be helpful for the removal company, friends and relatives.

Whom to tell. Besides friends and relatives, many other people have an interest in your whereabouts. You will find some of them in the checklist at 8.6. If you have lots of people to tell, it might be worthwhile have change-of-address cards printed or sending e-mails, giving your new address, telephone number and the date you will be moving.

Mains services. Your remover is not allowed to disconnect mains services. Make arrangements with your energy supplier well in advance to disconnect the cooker if you are taking it with you, and check that any other appliances can be easily disconnected on moving day. On the day, phone your energy supplier and give them a final reading, or you may be held responsible for power and fuel used until the next reading.

Telephone. Contact the telephone company providing the service to your new home and arrange to take over the service from the date of entry. If necessary, inform your internet service provider.

Deep freezer. Run down food stocks. Your remover will not accept responsibility for the contents.

Carpets and curtains. Check your quotation. Usually your remover will take down curtains and blinds and lift carpets if you ask for this to be included. They will not put them up again or re-lay fitted carpets.

System furniture. This can be a problem. Although designed to be dismantled and reassembled, in practice it may not reassemble so well. This type of problem cannot be covered by insurance.

Packing. How much the remover does depends on what you asked them to quote for. If you are paying for a complete service, leave it to them.

Insurance. See 8.3.

Special items. If you are concerned about items such as plants, IT equipment, antiques, fine art or a wine collection, discuss these is advance with your remover.

Don't take what you don't need. Treat your move as an opportunity for a ruthless sort out of unwanted possessions. Local charity shops welcome china, glass, books, ornaments, jewellery, pictures and good quality clothing, and some charitable organisations will take unwanted furniture and appliances to give to people who need them. Local volunteers will uplift cartons and sacks. If you have unwanted possessions that are not worth passing on, you should think about hiring a skip to dump them in, rather than leaving the new owner to deal with them.

8.5. Just before moving day

The following preparations will help you and your remover whether you are packing yourself or the remover is doing it for you.

China and glassware. Have crockery and glassware ready on a level surface for packing.

Drawers. Leave clothes and other light items in drawers but do not lock or over-fill them. Heavier items, such as books and tools, should be removed and packed separately.

Plan where things are going to go. Work out where you want your possessions to go in your new home. It will be helpful to draw a plan, give a copy to the remover's supervisor and make sure that someone will be there to show them where things are to go. Write in the names of the rooms on the plan and prepare labels for these rooms to go on boxes and furniture.

Make a note of what goes into boxes. As boxes are packed, label them with a description of their contents.

Parking. Warn your remover if there are any restrictions outside your new home. One removal van needs about 15 metres of parking space. It helps if the van can be parked close to the property.

Flats. If you are moving into a block of flats with a lift, you will need to arrange priority. If the lift is small or there isn't one, warn the removers in advance.

Unloading. Warn your removers about any hazards such as poor access, small doorways, and spiral staircases.

Spare key. If possible, give the supervisor a spare key, in case the van arrives before you do.

Children and pets. Try to arrange for friends or neighbours to look after young children or pets or both on the removal day.

Payment. Check the quotation for the remover's terms of payment. They may want payment in advance or a cheque or even cash on the removal day.

Important and valuable items. Gather together in one place the things you may need on the day of the move, such as keys, phone, cheque book, cash, map, telephone numbers of your solicitor and the removal firm, and so on.

The following preparations will be helpful to the new owner of your home.

- Look out instruction books and guarantees, and so on.

- Write out basic instructions about how to operate the central heating, security system, and so on.

- Pin up, in a prominent place, details of your new address and telephone number so that the new owner can contact you or pass them on to others trying to contact you.

8.6. Your responsibilities – a checklist of things that need to be done

The following checklist should be photocopied and pinned up in a prominent place.

• Confirm dates with remover

• Sign and return contract, with payment if required in advance

• Arrange insurance

• Arrange contact telephone number

• Dispose of unwanted possessions

• Start running down freezer contents

• Contact carpet fitters if needed

• Book mains services disconnections

• Take final meter readings

• Notify doctor, dentist, optician, vet

• Notify bank, building society, investment accounts

• Notify tax office

• Arrange final telephone bill and the take over of service in new home

• Notify internet service provider

• Arrange Royal Mail redirection

• Notify TV licensing and vehicle registration authorities

• Notify HP and credit firms

• Make local map for friends and remover

• Clear loft

• Organise parking at new home

• Plan where things are to go in new home

- Cancel milk and newspapers

- Clean out freezer

- Arrange minders for children and pets

- Find and label keys

- Gather together instructions for new owner

- Pin up details of new address and telephone number

- Send new-address cards to friends and relatives

- Separate trinkets, jewellery and small items

- Sort out linen and clothes

- Put garage/garden tools together

- Take down curtains and blinds

- Take down light fittings

- Collect children's toys

- Put together basic catering, including a kettle, for new home

- Put aside box or bag for important and valuable items

8.7. What to do if things go wrong

Things can and sometimes do go wrong in a complex operation such as moving home. You should at the least have adequate insurance cover. If you notice any breakages or damage before the removers leave, point them out to the supervisor, write the details on your contract and get him or her to initial them. Any of your possessions that are damaged or broken during the move should be kept for inspection by the company, or your insurers if you claim on the insurance policy. Make sure you claim within any specified time limit.

If you have a complaint about a removal company, write to it setting out your complaint and tell it what you expect it to do about it. If you are not satisfied with its response and the company is a member of the BAR, write to its Consumer Affairs

Manager (see 8.8). The BAR has conciliation and arbitration services to help resolve disputes with its members.

BAR conciliation and arbitration schemes

To use the conciliation scheme, write to the BAR giving details of your dispute. The BAR will give details to its member and ask for a response within 14 days. The BAR will then suggest a solution. If neither party accepts it, the matter can be referred to an arbitration scheme operated by the Chartered Institute of Arbitrators, independently of the BAR.

Under the arbitration scheme, you can claim for poor service but you cannot claim compensation for any amount more than £5,000, nor for physical injury or illness or the consequences of such injury or illness.

NGRS conciliation and ombudsman schemes

If you are not satisfied with the response to a complaint to a NGRS member, write to the NGRS Customer Services Department (see 8.8) giving details of your dispute. The NGRS will respond to you within ten days, give details to its member and ask for a response. The NGRS will then suggest a solution. If neither party accepts it, the matter can be referred to the Removals Ombudsman Scheme.

If you have a dispute that lies outwith the BAR conciliation and arbitration schemes or the Removals Ombudsman Scheme, or if it is with a removal company that is not a BAR or NGRS member, you should get legal advice.

8.8. Further information

For information about the services of the British Association of Removers, details of local BAR members or to make a complaint about a member, contact the British Association of Removers, Tangent House, 62 Exchange Road, Watford WD18 0TG (tel: 01923 699480, e-mail: info@bar.co.uk, http://www. removers.org.uk/).

For information about the National Guild of Removers and Storers, details of local NGRS members or to make a complaint about a member, contact the National Guild of Removers and Storers, 3 High Street, Chesham, Buckinghamshire HP5 1BG (tel: 01494 792279, e-mail: info@ngrs.co.uk, http://www. studiobasement.com/thinkbda/ngrs/moving_home.php).

Index

Note: Page numbers in **bold** indicate **major topics** and **contact details** for organisations and websites
Acts of Parliament *see* legislation

RICS *see* Royal Institution of
Chartered Surveyors
rights
to buy 11, 29, 45, 48
occupancy 40
of 'superior' 39
Royal Institution of Chartered
Surveyors 37, 60, 63-4
in Scotland **65**
running home *see* maintenance
Rural Home Ownership Grants 13, **29**

savings 56
scheme 1 survey (mortgage valuation)
44, 49-50, 59-60
scheme 2 survey (homebuyer's) 59,
60-1
Scotland's New Homebuyer 14
Scottish Consumer Council viii
Scottish Executive Environment and
Rural
Affairs Department 13
Scottish Legal Services Ombudsman
46, **47**
Scottish Solicitors' Discipline Tribunal
45
Scottish Solicitors' Property Centres **15**
search 46
fees 44
security, standard 40
self-employed, mortgage for 52-3
selling home **66-77**
advertising 69, 70, 71
after missives completed 73-5
closing date 71-2
complaints 76-7
marketing with agent 70-1
marketing without agent 68-9
offer, accepting 72-3
services (gas, electricity etc) 41-2
servitudes defined 39
settlement 41, 75
after 42-3
sewerage 22, 39
shared equity arrangement 7
shared ownership 12-13
sheltered housing (including
retirement) 2-3, 27

Sheltered Housing Code **30**
see also Age Concern
'snagging' 7
solicitor (or qualified conveyancer)
38-9, 70
complaints about 45-6, 76
fees 43-4, 45
information about 47
selling home 66, 68, 72, 75
and standard security 40
and title 35
see also Law Society
solicitors' property centres 15, 16, 38,
71
special treatments 20
stage payments 7, 36
stamp duty land tax 44-5, 47
standards, conversion and renovation **30**
storing furniture and goods 8-9, 79
structural survey 59, 62
'superior', rights of 39
Surveyor Ombudsman Scheme 64, **65**
Surveyors Arbitration Scheme **65**
surveys and valuations 15, 20, **59-65**
building 59, 62
complaints about 63-5
homebuyer's survey and valuation 59,
60-1
insurance 62-3
mortgage valuation report 44, 49-50,
59-60
offer 'subject to' 72
selling home 67, 69, 72
see also chartered surveyors

tax
Capital Gains 55
council 22, 75
and mortgages 53, 56
stamp duty land 44-5, 47
telephone and telecommunications
services 22, 81
television licence 22
tenements 25-6
Tenement Management Scheme 26,
28, 74
Tenements (Scotland) Act (2004) 26
see also factors; flats